MINI ENCYCLO
GUINEA PIGS
BREEDS & CARE

A guide to caring for your guinea pig

MYRA MAHONEY

INTERPET
PUBLISHING

Published by **Interpet Publishing,**
Vincent Lane,
Dorking,
Surrey RH4 3YX
England

© 2010 Interpet Publishing Ltd.

ISBN 9781842862261

Editor: **Hilary Russell**
Designer: **Sue Rose**
Photography: **Lyndon Nowell**

Production Management: **Colin Gower Enterprises Ltd.**

Printed in China

This book sets out to:

Provide a complete guide to every aspect of choosing and caring for your guinea pig, including housing, feeding, breeding and general health. It also provides a useful guide to the most popular breeds of guinea pig available to the pet owner. Health and Safety issues highlighted by the author should be heeded, particularly washing your hands after contact with your pet. In the case of illness it is advisable to seek the advice of a qualified veterinarian.

The information and recommendations in this book are given without any guarantees on behalf of the author and publisher, who disclaim any liability with the use of this material.

The Author

Myra Mahoney's affinity with guinea pigs started rather late in life, when she bought two of

these cuddly, good-tempered pets for two of her children as Easter presents. One morning, Myra found that the two sister guinea pigs (pink-eyed whites) has been joined by six little miniature guinea pigs. Myra says that these little creatures "exploded in my life and heart, where they have stayed ever since." This unexpected bonus led Myra to become deeply interested in keeping Cavies (the proper name for guinea pigs) and "the fancy." Myra then bought a Peruvian boar, Puff, and has been breeding and showing long-haired cavies ever since. Over the course of her showing career, Myra has won innumerable cups and trophies.

Myra has written this small book to share her forty years of experience with new guinea pig owners.

Contents

1 Understanding
your Guinea Pig PAGE 8

2 Choosing your
Guinea Pig PAGE 18

3 Feeding your Guinea Pig
PAGE 30

4 Housing your Guinea Pig
PAGE 36

5 Health, Hygiene and
Diseases PAGE 54

6 A—Z Guinea Pig Ailments PAGE 82

7 Showing your Guinea Pig PAGE 98

8 Guinea Pig Nursery PAGE 114

9 Breeds of Exhibition Cavies PAGE 124

Index PAGE 206

LEFT: *Guinea pigs have many fans.*   RIGHT: *Chocolate Dalmation*

1 • *Understanding Your Guinea Pig*

What is a guinea pig?

The guinea pig or cavy we have as a pet today is from the vast family known as Rodents, which also includes rats, mice, gerbils, hamsters and chinchillas. This name means to gnaw, and all rodents have one major characteristic in common: long, constantly-growing incisor teeth at the front, two at the top and two at the bottom of the jaw. These are used for gnawing and breaking off pieces of food. Guinea pigs also have a pair of premolars (top and bottom) either side at the back of the mouth, and finally three pairs of molars (top and bottom) which grind down the food transferred to the back of the mouth by the tongue. This makes twenty in all, and very effective they are too – cavies are always eating! Most pet owners, and even some breeders, have never seen back teeth, as there is a large gap between these and the incisors, filled by the very fleshy insides of the cheeks. If you dare, you can insert a little finger right to the back of the cavy's mouth and, by pressing down gently, feel the sharp points of the premolars.

During my research, I came across an enormous amount of contradictory information about where guinea pigs originate and how they got their name. When finally my brain could take no more Latin names, I decided to give the facts on which all experts agree in an easy-to-understand format:

• All the present-day guinea pigs originated at least 3000 years ago in South America. There are seven species of the genus Cavia,

ABOVE:*Cavies are always eating!*

our own cavy being *Cavia porcellus* "pig-like cavy." It is thought that it is likened to a pig because, when hairless, its body shape is similar to that of a sucking pig, it makes "winking" noises like a piglet and it roots and snuffles around in search of food in a similar manner to a pig.

• From 1200–1532AD, the Incas produced a variety of strains bred for colour, pattern and "flavour." Many sources tell you that only the agouti-patterned cavies come from South America and that they were not selectively bred until they reached Europe in the 16th century, but the Incas got there before us in breeding different varieties.

OPPOSITE: *There are no known colonies of "our" cavies (Cavia porcellus) breeding in the wild today.*

- The cavy is still widely kept as a source of food by the native people of Peru, Ecuador and Bolivia. In some villages they are kept in huts, just as we keep chickens in chicken coops. In other areas they are allowed free range to scavenge. Where this occurs, some feral populations of guinea pigs have been established, but apparently there are no known colonies of "our" cavies (Cavia porcellus) breeding in the wild today. Wild cavies still reside in a wide range of habitats all over South America, including open grasslands, forest edges, rocky areas and even swamps, where they are known to swim. They have been found at elevations up to 4200m. These wild cavies are known to the natives of South America as restless cavies, possibly because they are always busy and never seem to sleep.

- When the Spanish conquered the Incas in the 16th century, domesticated cavies were brought back to Europe by way of Guinea on the west coast of Africa, a possible explanation for the name. They came to England in the middle of the 17th century, and so began the close association with humans that did not end up with them on a plate! In Great Britain, mainland Europe, Australia and the United States, we enjoy them as much-loved pets, which has led to a thriving fancy.

Anatomy of a guinea pig

On careful inspection from top to toe, you will see that, in addition to the long, sharp teeth,

ABOVE: *When hairless, like this Skinny, its body shape is similar to that of a suckling pig.*

ABOVE: *The long incisor teeth at the front, two at the top and two at the bottom of the jaw, are constantly growing.*

ABOVE: *The eyes are placed on the side of the head so that enemies can be seen from above and behind, as well as in front.*

your pet has:

Nose: A soft, inquisitive nose, with a strong sense of smell. The guinea pig will get to know your smell and that of your close friends and relations.

Eyes: Bright, round eyes that hardly ever blink or close. Guinea pigs are known to close their eyes in sleep for no longer than 10 minutes at a time, so alert are they to danger. The eyes are placed on the side of the head so that enemies can be seen from above and behind, as well as in front. The long eyebrows are

sensitive, like the whiskers.

Ears: Large, drooping, petal-shaped ears that can hear the faintest sound. Try rustling a plastic carrier bag when you are a long distance away, and wait for the shrill "peep-peeping" to start.

Whiskers: Like a cat's, the guinea pig';s whiskers are used to feel how much room there is to squeeze through holes.

Mouth: A cavernous mouth with 20 teeth.

Body: A large, plump body, consisting mostly of belly, more bulbous at the back end than at the

ABOVE: *Hair covers the entire body, except behind each ear, where there is a large, bald patch.*

front.

Hair (not fur): This covers the entire body, except behind each ear, where there is a large, bald patch. This is a useful place in which to begin looking for unwelcome visitors in the form of parasites. If you see your pet scratching behind his ear, investigate at once. The ears themselves are hairless.

Tail: You will have been told that a guinea pig has no tail but, if you feel your guinea pig's rear end, you will find a little stump where, thousands of years ago, his ancestor would have had quite a large one. Evolution and lack of use have made it disappear, just as our arms have grown shorter now that we do not have to swing through the trees.

Grease gland: A grease gland is situated at the rear end, used for scenting territory and other pigs. This is quite smelly.

Nipples: Two nipples or teats can be found on the belly. Females have these for suckling their young. Males, like human males, have them too, for no apparent reason.

Underbelly: A furry underbelly, very susceptible to being squeezed by the tiny fingers of small children. It contains all the important organs of the body except the heart and lungs, which are protected by the rib cage in the chest.

Legs: Two front legs, short and set fairly close together, and two back legs, set wider apart. These are longer than the front ones. The front feet have leathery pads and four tiny toes with a sharp claw on each toe, sometimes used for holding food down to eat it more easily. Cavies never pick food up between the paws like squirrels and chinchillas do. The back legs are strong, with leathery pads right up to the heel, and each foot has three toes, with bigger and thicker claws than on the front feet. Because of this, guinea pigs can push off and run at great speed when feeling threatened. So be warned – your pet will be there one second, and gone the next!

Guinea Pig Language

The sound for which the guinea pig is most noted is the loud, rising, high-pitched "wheeping" that greets the owner at feed time. Noises associated with food, such as the opening of a food bin lid or the rustling of a bag, trigger off this delightful sound – although all my cavies sounding off at once in my shed produce cacophony rather than harmony! The strange thing is that, if I go into the caviary when it is not food time, they do not make a single "wheep." According to my research, cavies are capable of making 11 different sounds, but none of my sources tells me what they all are. These are the twelve different calls and utterances that mine make, with my interpretation of them:

1 The aforementioned "wheeping." This is definitely a demanding sound, on a high, rising note. Guinea pigs keep it up till they get what they want.

2 A "wheeping" slightly lower in tone is made by cavies greeting each other.

ABOVE: A "wheeping" slightly lower in tone is made by cavies greeting each other.

3 An even lower "wheeping" is made when you attempt to touch a cavy who doesn't want to be picked up or touched. This has a really grumpy tone.

4 An anxious, high-pitched "wheeping" is made by a baby separated from its mother.

5 A "chuck-chucking" call made by a mother to call her babies around her to be fed or have their bottoms cleaned.

6 A loud shriek on a falling note indicates that a cavy is hurt-perhaps being picked on by another one or catching a claw in the bars of the cage.

7 When courting a sow, the boar makes a purring sound on a low note, accompanied by what I call a "war dance." He moves around the sow slowly as he shifts his weight from one back foot to the other. Sows also display this behaviour with other sows when they come into season.

8 When accepting a boar, the sow emits a high-pitched "chuttering" sound and pretends that she is not really interested.

9 Teeth chattering, accompanied by a sideways "war dance," heralds a head-to-head between two boars. This is the signal to put some heavy gloves on to separate them, or throw a towel over them. A huge yawn before the head-to-head does not mean that the boar is tired or disinterested – it is a way of showing the opposition what a fine set of

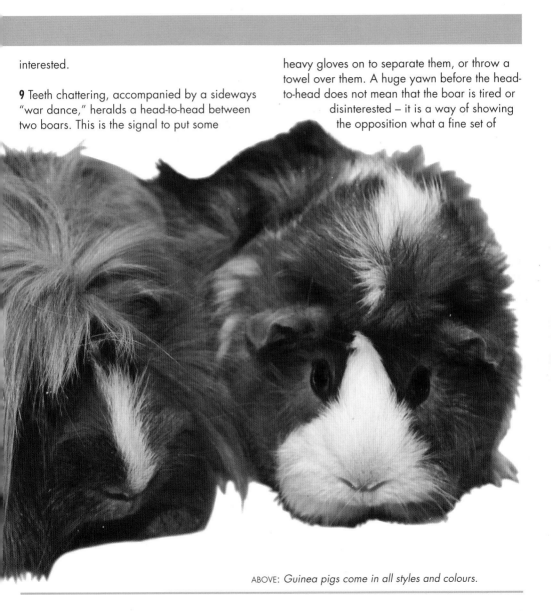

ABOVE: *Guinea pigs come in all styles and colours.*

ABOVE: *Guinea pigs are enjoyed by young and old alike.*

all activities are resumed.

12 This last sound is legendary in the fancy, and no-one seems able to give a reason for it. Anyone keeping just a few pets will probably never hear it, and in 40 years I have heard it no more than a dozen times. It usually happens when I am busy in the shed and the cavies are all contentedly bustling around their cages. The peace is suddenly shattered by a bird-like cheeping, all on one note and getting louder and louder. A complete silence comes over the whole shed as everyone, including me, freezes to the spot. When I get over the shock, I try to find the guinea pig who is making this strange, ethereal sound by moving slowly in the direction of the noise. The culprit is not hard to identify: all the others are flattened on the floor with wide eyes, while the "singer" is upright with his neck stretched and sometimes with one or both front feet lifted. My appearance in front of the cage does not seem to faze him – he goes on with his strange cheeping until he is finished. The whole episode only lasts for 20 seconds or so. The chirper is nearly always an adolescent boar and my theory is that he is experiencing a

teeth he is up against.

10 My favourite sound is a low, bubbly murmuring among a group of guinea pigs, contentedly munching their way through the goodies I have just put in their cage.

11 The above sound is sometimes interrupted if I drop something or sneeze. Then a low "chuttering" will go around the shed like a Mexican wave, followed by complete silence. When nothing dreadful happens, latent urge to voice the alarm call used by his ancestors thousands of years ago, before domestication bred out the need for it, rendering sentinels unnecessary. I call it the "sentinel" sound.

Body language

If your guinea pig throws his head back when you stroke it, he is not asking you to do it again – he is saying, "Get off!" If you don't do as he says, he will get very annoyed.

Many guinea pigs like to be tickled under the chin and lift their heads higher and higher as you do so, closing their eyes with a blissful look.Some like their heads scratched, especially behind the ears.

Coprophagy

If you see your guinea pig duck his head under his belly and take one of his droppings from his anus to munch on it, do not be disgusted – this is perfectly normal and necessary behaviour. A cavy's digestive system does not extract all the necessary vitamins the first time round, so special soft pellets are made, containing the B vitamins and bacteria that inhabit the flora in the gut. The cavy re-ingests these, just as a cow does when it chews the cud. If your guinea pig ever becomes so ill that he cannot do this, you must supplement his diet with Brewers Yeast tablets (dose: two daily) until he is better.

LEFT: *Many guinea pigs like to be tickled under the chin*

2 • *Choosing Your Guinea Pig*

ABOVE: *Two Teddies*
OPPOSITE: *A proud young owner with her cavy.*

One or more guinea pigs?

Guinea pigs are social animals who live in small herds in the wild. This puts them among the few rodents who simply must have the companionship of another of their kind to be entirely happy. Without another guinea pig to talk to and exchange pleasantries with, a cavy will become withdrawn and lonely. Even the constant companionship of a human, with all the love you can give, cannot replace the special bond between two or more guinea

pigs. Many times have I seen a cavy that has been an only pet introduced to another, and the change that comes over the lone one is incredible and a joy to see.

So, now that (hopefully) I have persuaded you to have two, where should you get them from?

• A reputable pet shop would seem the obvious choice. Before you buy, make sure that the shop is clean and the animals are healthy, with plenty of food and hay in the cages.

- Some breeders advertise in pet shops where animals are not for sale, or the pet shop owner may have the name and address of a local breeder. The breeder is by far the best choice, as he or she will send you away with all the advice you need to start off and will nearly always welcome you back if you have any problems.

- If you are lucky enough to have a friend with baby guinea pigs that are unwanted, you will be able to offer them a good home.

- Guinea pig rescue sanctuaries are always looking for good homes for unwanted pets. Telephone your local RSPCA for details.

Male guinea pigs (boars) or female guinea pigs (sows)?

I am pleased to be able to use this opportunity to dispel the widespread myth perpetrated by almost every book on the subject that you cannot keep two boars together. In my experience, two sows are often far more argumentative. They get on well most of the time but, when one is in season, she is bad-tempered and the other one has to keep

ABOVE: *Selfs sit quietly in the judging box at a show.*

out of the way until it is over. The season occurs every 16 days, and one or the other could be quarrelsome on her "off day" for at least 24 hours. Of course, this is not always the case – some sows never argue. With boars, two litter-brothers will always be friends and, if boars from two different litters are put together at weaning time, they will always get on. An adult boar will take on orphan baby boars and weaned boars if the smell of the mother is removed with a bath, and I have even paired two older

LEFT: *A litter of four day old cavies with their Alpaca mother.*

boars when the companion of one has died. Sometimes the first introduction is not successful, for it seems that, when older boars meet for the first time, they either love or hate each other. It becomes apparent within 10 minutes, sometimes only 10 seconds, whether they are going to become friends. If not, try again with a different one. You will have success eventually. I have four adult boars living free-range together on the floor of my shed, and they couldn't be happier. Although they can talk to sows through the mesh of the bottom cages (and sometimes get very excited) they do not get antagonistic to each other. They snuggle together for warmth very contentedly at night in their little house.

In a stud like mine, there are always stud boars past their "sell-by" date and too old for breeding, and I pair these up to live out their old age. I am pleased when one of my visitors

falls in love with a pair of pensioners; it's wonderful to see them go off to a good home.

If you want a boar and sow to live together without starting a family, or if the sow is too old for babies, there is no need to put either through the stress of neutering, with the risk of anaesthetic, which is very dangerous for cavies. There are always less drastic ways around the problem. You could set up a cage with a wire mesh partition in the middle, so that they could talk without touching. The same applies if two guineas of the same sex just will not get on together.

The smell of a sow could make two otherwise friendly boars fight, so always wash your hands after handling females and scrub hutches that have previously housed sows before housing boars in them.

So either boars or sows make wonderful pets.

ABOVE: *Saffron Self Gloucester*

Which breed?

There are over 30 different breeds from which to choose, with new ones appearing nearly every year. Cross-bred guinea pigs come in any combination and colour of these breeds, so the choice is vast. Whether you go to a breeder for a particular colour or coat type or buy a cross-breed from a breeder, pet shop or guinea pig rescue sanctuary is your choice. If you write to the Southern Cavy Club or the National Cavy Club of Great Britain enclosing a stamped, addressed envelope for a reply,

either organisation will send you a welcome pack and supply you with the names, addresses and telephone numbers of the breeders in your area.

SELFS (all one colour) are smooth, short-coated cavies. They come in the following colours:
- Black
- White (pink- or dark-eyed)
- Cream
- Chocolate
- Golden (pink- or dark-eyed)

- Red (mahogany)
- Lilac
- Beige
- Buff (dark cream)
- Saffron (pale yellow)
- Slate (blue/grey)

NON-SELFS (anything that is not a self, including long-hairs) come in most of the self colours, or a combination of them, and include:

Abbysinian (short and rough-coated, with up to eight rosettes all over the body)

Agouti (ticked, smooth hairs, making the guinea pig look speckled)

Crested (smooth, with crest on its head)

Satin (smooth, shining satin coat)

Dutch (smooth, markings like Dutch rabbit in white and one other colour)

Tortoiseshell (smooth with black and red chequered effect)

Tortoiseshell-and-white (smooth, with black, red and white chequered effect)

Roan (smooth, with coloured hairs evenly mingled with white)

Rex (short, curly-coated)

Dalmation – not Dalmatian, like the dog – (smooth white with coloured spots)

ABOVE: *Abyssinian Agouti*

HIMALAYAN (smooth white with chocolate or black nose, feet and ears)

- Peruvian (long-coated, hair falls over face and around body)

- Sheltie (long-coated, hair growing backward from head and around body)

- Coronet (a sheltie with a crest on its head)

- Texel (a rexed sheltie, making the long coat fall in ringlets)

- Merino (a rexed coronet)

- Alpaca (a rexed Peruvian)

If the eventual size is a consideration, it would be as well for you to know that rexes and long-hairs grow slightly larger than the other breeds. Long-hairs take a little more time and trouble but, on the whole, they groom themselves and, if the coat is trimmed regularly to keep it off the floor, they will only need a weekly brush and comb to make very attractive pets. I keep a few short-haired smooth and

ABOVE: *This is a Coronet with its head crest.*

ABOVE: *This is a Texel with its kinked coat.*
BELOW: *An Alpaca groomed for showing.*

ABOVE: *A "hairy" Alpaca!*

Reputable breeders will not usually let Dalmation or Roan cavies go to pet homes. This is because of a lethal gene that exists in these breeds, which could cause terrible deformities in the offspring of a Roan bred to a Roan or a Dalmation to a Dalmation.

Author Peter Gurney has written a very useful book about guinea pig breeds. It is called "What's My Guinea Pig?" and is full of wonderful photographs of pure- and cross-bred guinea pigs. This could help you to choose.

"The Fancy"

Those belonging to the cavy "Fancy" are dedicated to breeding and improving the many different varieties of guinea pig on exhibition at shows today. There are clubs catering for specific breeds and local clubs whose members get together regularly and hold shows. All of these are catered for by umbrella clubs such as the Southern Cavy Club, the National Cavy Club and the Scottish National Cavy Club. If you feel you would like to know more about showing your pets, you can find the addresses of these clubs in the Addresses section.

Your guinea pigs do not have to be pure-bred to be shown. There are pet classes for cross-breeds too, with the emphasis on pet. Judges like guineas that are obviously used to being handled, so the more laid back your pet, the more likely it is to get a prize card and rosette. There is also a small amount of prize money, but this rarely covers your entry fee.

Starting off in showing often leads to bigger

rough-coated pigs because people seem to shy away from long-hairs but, when visitors come for the cross-breeds, they invariably leave with a couple of "hairies."

If long-hairs are to be shown, the coat must be allowed to grow long from the day it is born, and the hair folded up in wrappers to keep it from getting tangled and dirty. If the coat is spoiled in any way you will have to start over again with another baby. The hair grows at the rate of 2–3cm a month, so non-show pigs will have to be trimmed periodically to keep them tidy.

ABOVE: *A "Hairy!"*

things and certainly introduces you to a hobby where life-long friendships can be made. Great fun is had by all, young and old alike, and cavy fanciers agree that when they are all together is the only time that they feel really normal. After keeping guinea pigs seriously for some time, wait for the reaction when you have to tell other people what you do at the weekends – they'll think you are completely mad. Little do they know that you are kept saner than anyone because of the therapeutic effect your endearing little charges have on your life.

LEFT: *Guinea pigs can keep you sane.*

RIGHT: *This Marten Sable shows his tummy in the arms of a show judge.*

3 • *Feeding Your Guinea Pig*

ABOVE: *Guinea pigs need Vitamin C from their greens!*

Guinea pigs are herbivores, which means that they do not eat anything but vegetable matter. They need a meal of fresh vegetables and fruit every day to supply Vitamin C. Like monkeys, apes, and humans, they have a daily need for this essential vitamin.

Vegetable matter, whether bought or foraged, this must be:
- Unfrozen
- Clean
- Free from contamination by crop spraying, animal droppings, exhaust fumes and so on

ABOVE: *These Gloucesters are tucking into a grassy snack.*

- Fresh (no yellowing to cause tummy upsets)
- Mildew-free

If you are unable to give your pets vegetables for a day or two you can add Vitamin C to their water. A small piece of a 1000mg soluble Vitamin C tablet broken off and added to the water bottle will suffice. This vitamin cannot be overdosed as what the body does not absorb will be flushed away at the other end.

Hay

This is absolutely essential. They eat very large quantities every day. It acts as roughage, aiding digestion (I call it "lining the stomach")

and gives them constant nibbling material. This is necessary to keep their ever-growing teeth worn down. Buy good quality hay from a farmer or pet shop. It must be soft, sweet, and free of mould and thistles.

Cereal mixes

There are several good mixes especially formulated for guinea pigs, some containing Vitamin C. This should never be used as a replacement for fresh vegetables as:

- Vitamin C added to any product has a very short shelf life.
- Guinea pigs thrive on variety in the form of vegetables, fruit, salad and wild plants.

31

ABOVE: *There are several good mixes especially formulated for guinea pigs.*

Do not use hamster mixes, as peanuts and sunflower seeds are not suitable, or rabbit mixes containing ACS (an anti-coccidiosis medication), as this is toxic to guinea pigs.

Do add to your dry mix as a change from time to time pasture mix for horses, fibre mix for horses or goats and herb blends for horses. Some of these contain molasses, much relished by guinea pigs. I use additional alfalfa in the form of pellets or fibre mix.

Water

This must be available at all times. Always flush out any water remaining in the bottle before refilling it. Guinea pigs have a disgusting habit of blowing leftover food from their cheeks back into the tube and fouling the water. Clean the bottles with a bottle brush and the tube with a pipe-cleaner regularly.

Do not use a bowl for water. Your pet will either use it as a toilet or tip it over and soak its cage.

Cultivated vegetables

The following are enjoyed by guinea pigs and give sufficient amounts of Vitamin C:

- **Cauliflower leaves** – you can eat the heart, as your pet will not be so keen.
- **Cabbage** – the white, crisp kind used for coleslaw will only be eaten under sufferance, if there is nothing else.
- **Broccoli**
- **Sprout tops and stalks** – not the sprouts, use them yourself.
- **Spinach** – only one or two leaves a week, as they contain oxalic acid.
- **Chicory**
- **Sweetcorn** – silks and leaves too.
- **Runner beans** – the whole bean, but not the plant.
- **Pea pods**
- **Carrots** – the all-time favourite.
- **Beetroot** – served raw and quartered (they will not eat the skin).
- **Swede** – an acquired taste, but persevere, as it is high in Vitamin C.
- **Turnips and parsnips** – again, will only be eaten if there is nothing else, but do try.

Salad vegetables

All the following are loved by guineas but have a relatively low Vitamin C content. Give as treats but do not use as a staple diet.

- **Cucumber**

ABOVE: *Salads are treats rather than staple foods.*

- **Celery**
- **Lettuce** in all its forms – contains laudanum, so give in moderation. Romaine lettuce is safe
- **Red and green peppers** – without the seeds.
- **Tomatoes** – liked by some.

Potato peelings

Potatoes in their raw form are a definite no-no but, if you want to see your pets tuck into a dish of food with real enthusiasm, cook off some potato peelings, drain them and cool them. Mix them with a handful of broad bran, place the mash in the cage – and stand back from the rush! My children used to love to pinch it out of the saucepan before it got to the guineas.

ABOVE: *Cavy pellets*

33

Photograph by Sue Rose

ABOVE: *Grass – the Guinea Pig's favourite foodstuff.*

Fruits

In order of preference:
- **Apples and pears**.
- **Melon**.
- **Grapes** – seedless, or with pips removed.
- **Bananas** – including skin.
- **Oranges** – in segments, with skin on.
- **Cherries** – remove stones first.

Peaches and plums are too acidic and could cause mouth scabs. Too much fruit of any kind can cause scabbing, so do not be too generous with it.

Wild plants

Any of the following can be given in small quantities. As most wild plants have some kind of medicinal quality you can easily overdose on any of them. Give a mixture of wild plant foods, and not large amounts of any one thing.

- **Dandelions** – a laxative and diuretic (stimulates the kidneys to work harder), but a small amount every day, mixed with grass and always accompanied by hay, can be a valuable tonic.
- **Grass** – their favourite food of all, but do not give mowings, which heat up quickly and contain moss, fungi and poisonous plants.
- **Parsley** – a most useful herb. Eaten readily by convalescing or poorly guinea pigs, pregnant sows and mothers with babies, it is highly nutritious and rich in Vitamin C.
- **Clover** – a good conditioner.
- **Strawberry leaves** – good for checking scours if you can persuade the guinea pigs to eat them.
- **Shepherd's Purse** – has astringent qualities. Will be eaten readily by scouring guinea pigs, but healthy ones do not seem keen.
- **Sow thistle** – good for nursing sows, with its milky-white sap. Do not give when the stem is woody.
- **Plantain** – broad leaf and narrow leaf are both good. They have astringent qualities, so give with Dandelion.

These are just a few of the wild plants that are safe and most easily recognisable. There is a very old saying that has been my motto throughout my life with guineas and has never failed me: "If in doubt – leave it out!"

Poisonous plants
WILD PLANTS:

Here is a list of the very poisonous wild plants, in alphabetical order: anemone, arum, autumn crocus, belladonna (deadly nightshade), bindweed (convolvulus), black nightshade, bluebell, bryony (white and black), buttercup, celandine, corn cockle, daisy, docks, dog mercury, elder, figwort, flags and irises, fool's parsley, foxglove, hemlock, henbane, oak, poppy, scarlet pimpernel (this is nearly always found growing near chickweed, which is why I have not included chickweed on my safe list), spurge, toad flax, and travellers' joy (old man's beard).

GARDEN PLANTS:

Here is a list of poisonous plants to be found in the garden: acacia, aconite, beech, box, Christmas rose (hellebore – autumn and winter), Lenten rose (spring), columbine, daffodil (and all plants grown from bulbs), gypsophila, hyacinth, ivy (and berries), laburnum, larkspur or delphinium, lily of the valley, lobelia, love in a mist, potato tops, privet, rhubarb leaves, snowdrop, scarlet runner (foliage), yew.

And finally...

Last but not least: a good old standby for any under-the-weather guineas, mums (before and after littering) and babies, is brown bread and milk in a flat saucer.

Happy munching!

BELOW: *Carrots – always popular!*

Photograph by Sue Rose

4 • *Housing Your Guinea Pig*

OPPOSITE AND ABOVE: *Indoor units*

Caged Guinea Pigs

You must make sure you have your guinea pig house ready and waiting before you bring your new pets home. It could be a hutch in the garden for summer accommodation (May to September) that could be over-wintered in the garage or shed (September to May). Alternatively, you can use an indoor cage with a plastic tray and wire cage top. If the garage is to be their winter home, it is essential not to start up the car inside the garage, as carbon monoxide fumes and gas from car exhausts are just as lethal to cavies as to humans.

A hutch should be as large as you can manage, but allowing an area of at least 0.2 m² (2ft²) per guinea pig. Therefore, for two guinea pigs, a minimum of 90cm (3ft) across by 60cm (2ft) from front to back and not much more than 40cm (16in) high would be ideal. Cavies do not like too much space above their heads; they feel more secure in a low-roofed cage. One end should be sectioned off as a bedroom for them to hide in and get away from bad weather. The roof should be rain-proofed and sloping from front to back. The roof will also need to be 5cm (2in) larger all around than the hutch to give protection against severe weather. A plastic or weather-proof sheet weighted with a length of wood at the bottom should be attached to the front of the roof so that it can be dropped down at night and in very bad weather. The doors should be fastened with bolts as well as just catches as foxes and dogs are past masters at opening doors. By the same token, the mesh should be fastened very securely to the doors. Foxes and even weasels, rats and stoats are very good at demolishing wire mesh.

I would be happier if guinea pigs were never kept outside, but I know this is unrealistic in the face of the tradition that rabbits and guinea pigs have always been kept in hutches in the garden. I can only advise that they should

OPPOSITE AND ABOVE: *Outside units*

ABOVE: *Long run*

BELOW: *Grazing guinea pig*

never be out in the winter. Damp, cold and draughts are the biggest killers of guineas and, living outside, they are susceptible to all three.

In the summer, the hutch must be somewhere that is always shaded from the sun. Heatstroke is a real danger and even a big run can be a death-trap if you do not notice the sun moving around and they have no shade to escape to.

If your guinea pigs are kept in a shed, it must be well ventilated but warm in the winter and airy but cool in the summer. If the shed has the sun on it at any time during the day it would help if you have a screen door made and mesh at the windows to keep vermin, foxes, dogs and cats out. Although direct draughts are bad,

ABOVE: *Outside units*

ABOVE: *Outside arc* RIGHT: *Montgomery*

you must have circulation of air, and I use an oscillating fan on the hottest days.

If your pets are going to live in the house, a hygienic and easy to clean option is the wire-topped tray. These come in different sizes, but the ideal is 90cm x 60crn for two or more guinea pigs. It has an opening in the side and also one in the top for easy removal of the guineas. The wire top unclips for easy cleaning

out and you can use it to pop over the guineas on the grass or on the floor while you are cleaning their trays.

Never put your guinea pig on a mesh or wire-bottomed cage of the type used by some rabbit owners. A cavy's feet are not suited to these floors and dreadful accidents can occur, resulting in a lame guinea pig.

For both hutches and indoor cages, a quick

ABOVE: *Indoor cage*

and easy means of bedding is a thick layer of newspaper, clean wood shavings (not sawdust) or shredded paper and several large handfuls of hay (not straw). The hay must be replaced every day, as it will be eaten. Never, at any time, must your guinea pigs be without hay.

Buy a heavy, flat-bottomed ceramic food dish and a water-bottle that clips on to the cage. Drinking water must always be available, as water in a dish will soon become murky with bedding. Once it is contaminated in this way, the cavies will not drink it.

Put a log from a fruit tree, such as apple or pear, inside the cage. Other fruit trees, such as cherry and plum, have saps that cause tummy upsets. Some guineas enjoy gnawing these logs – others ignore them. In the play area of the hutch you could place a house brick or breeze block. Cavies love to sit or lie on these and, in the summer, they are cool. When they do not want to rest, they use them to jump up and down on. This is good exercise for them – a guinea pig stepping block.

A run or grazing ark in the garden is

essential for them to exercise and graze for a few hours each day in the summer months (end of May to the beginning of September). They love to be busy and you will hear them making a bigger variety of noises than usual when they have a large play area. The ideal scenario in fine weather is an enclosed area of the garden in which the hutch, with a ramp up to its door, can be placed and the children can play with the guinea pigs. All kinds of set-ups can be made to test their abilities, including a maze and tunnels with drainage pipes. However, this is not possible without the cooperation of a "handy" relation.

A word of warning about wet tummies. Never put guineas out on grass until the earth has warmed (around the end of May), and then only towards the end of the morning, when the grass is dry. Make sure you bring them in before the evening dew makes the grass wet again. Watch also for strong winds at ground level and supply an upturned wooden box with a cavy-sized hole in its side in which they can shelter if necessary. Stop putting them out at the end of August. Many pets die of pneumonia during summer as a result of getting wet and chilled in their runs.

Indoor Free-Rangers

I have not been able to enjoy the pleasure of allowing my guinea pigs free range of the house as my usually long-suffering husband is allergic to hay, and having it indoors causes him untold misery. No hay, no guinea pigs! If I bring them in for a bath, they come in on towels in a box and are quickly dried and put back in the shed again as soon as possible. The shed is heated and kept at 10°C (50°F) in the winter, so their brief house visit does not cause too much of a temperature change. When I get a water heater in the shed they will not have to come indoors at all. However, I do have several friends who have house guineas and one couple have given me a detailed

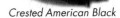

Crested American Black

report on their behaviour. They had two of my Peruvian boars a year ago.

Free-range guinea pigs do not make ideal pets for the house proud as, however hard you try to keep the floor clean, there will always be hay trailed about, plus the odd few droppings scattered on the carpet. It is possible to train guineas to use a litter tray, but in general a guinea pig's motto is, "When you gotta go you gotta go!" – wherever you are at the time. However, if you are tolerant, they make fascinating and enjoyable free-range pets, as long as you are aware of their presence under your feet all the time and are constantly aware of the dangers lurking in the safest of houses.

It would be dangerous to have cavies on the loose when very small children are about. You have only to see a toddler chasing pigeons in the park to imagine what sport they would have with guinea pigs. The child is only having fun, and it would be wrong to put temptation in his or her way.

Litter trays: A cat litter tray lined with newspaper and hay works well if you add a little soiled hay and some of their droppings every time you change it. This will encourage them to continue to use it. Debbie finds that they are more inclined to use a tray that has been placed in a dark corner, such as under a coffee table. They also spend a lot of time outside the tray, lying close to it, so Debbie puts the tray on a piece of washable, rubber-backed carpet. In case of accidents elsewhere, she washes the area with a vinegar and water solution, which seems to discourage them from using the spot again.

ABOVE: *A Peruvian*

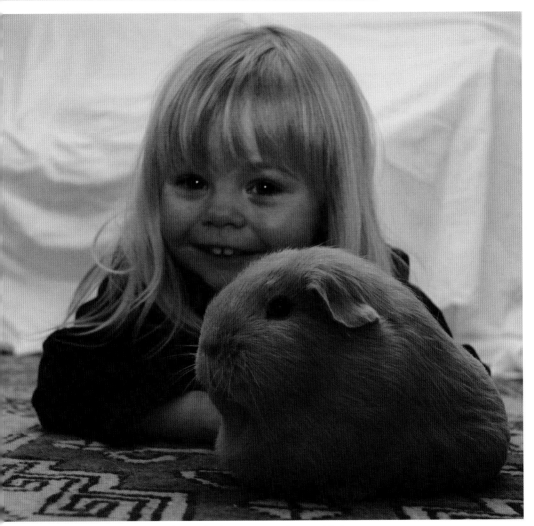

ABOVE: *They make fascinating and enjoyable free-range pets.*

ABOVE: *Do owners look like their guinea pigs?*

Chewing loose wires is a temptation, especially telephone wires, but these can be covered with tubing such as that used for siphoning fish tanks, obtainable in any lengths from aquarist stores. If wires are kept off the floor and hidden, the guineas soon forget they are there. One friend covered her telephone wires with a telephone directory, which they found particularly delectable and, when she removed the directory, they chased after it, forgetting the wires. Books and newspapers left within their reach will have a very short reading life but most owners have never had any trouble with them chewing furniture, and there is plenty of

opportunity in her house. They love to weave in and out of the dining table and chair legs – a mini-guinea slalom! Under the dining table is a favourite sleeping place, and that is where they run to with a tasty morsel they wish to keep to themselves.

Cage: A friend's indoor cage is made from a wooden rabbit hutch with a front-opening door and a hatch. It is painted in coordinating colours to match the living room. With the hatch open, the guinea pigs can come and go as they wish. Their main meals, hay and water bottles are there, although they are also hand fed titbits and treats. They also have a safe haven to run to if something frightens them, such as the telephone ringing (a noise they seem to hate), or a stranger visiting. They still, however, choose to doze under the dining table.

Two's company

The importance of having more than one guinea pig becomes obvious when you observe guinea pig behaviour at close quarters. While one dozes, the other keeps careful watch and when my friend holds one on her lap on the sofa, the other is at her feet, and they are constantly calling to each other. While playing and exploring, they run around in single file like a two-carriage train and,

wherever one goes, the other follows. They get used to things being in the same place all the time and if anything strange appears (slippers, for example) they are inclined to bump into them. This must echo the instincts of wild cavies in their natural habitat, where they use well-trodden tracks in the long grass, just as deer use trails through the woods in this country.

Guineas love tunnels, and my friend creates a maze of them with cushions, boxes, books and so on. They hide away and then, one at a time, make lightning quick forays into the

A grassy treat!

49

middle of the room, returning to report to the other, or dash back and forth from under the television trolley to under the dining table, just as if they were in the wild dashing from one clump of bush to another.

I envy my friend the joy of living with her guineas at hand all the time. She's a glutton for punishment and has just taken two "old boys" from me (Peruvians again). They are in the process of being integrated into the household by being placed in their cages on the floor so that the two residents can talk to them through the bars. I am informed that the youngsters spend all day trying to break them out of prison! I am looking forward to a progress report.

Favourite foods

Having your guineas indoors gives them a definite advantage as far as treats are concerned. Their sense of smell tells them when their favourite foods are being prepared in the kitchen and their loud "wheeping" as soon as a cucumber is cut makes it impossible for you to carry on preparing your salads without giving them some. Debbie used to block off the kitchen entrance to stop them from getting into dangerous places but she soon found that they treat the doorway and the change from carpet to tiles as a boundary not to be crossed. They stand inside the lounge and lean across the line to see what is going on in the kitchen.

Their favourite time of the day is when my

LEFT: *Two's company!*

51

ABOVE: *Place caged guinea pigs close together and they can become friends.*

friend's husband comes home from the golf course with a bag of grass. They hear the car before Debbie does and rush into the middle of the room, "wheeping" loudly, until Paddy comes through the door and gives them the bag – it never fails. They have been dreadfully

ABOVE: *An indoor guinea pig is an entertaining companion!*

spoiled, with firm, red apples the favourite of one (they will not eat soft, green ones) and sweet pears the favourite of the other (hard ones are rejected). One likes spring greens and the other prefers curly kale – and so it goes on. Other favourites are dandelions, cauliflower trimmings and, of course, carrots. These are always around to be nibbled on, as Debbie is very aware that salad treats do not contain enough vitamin C to supply their daily requirement.

A word of warning: If you have indoor free-rangers, be careful of house-plants and cut flowers. Many can prove fatal to guinea pigs, so keep trailing plants out of reach and, when cut flowers begin to drop, make sure they are not accessible to foraging pets.

53

5 • *Health, Hygiene and Diseases*

I was eight when I was allowed my first pet, a little pink mouse called "Pinky." My parents were not really pet-oriented, and left the care of Pinky to me. I loved him to bits, and spent hours playing with him. One day, the family went to the beach and, when we got home, the poor little thing was dead in his cage in the conservatory, which must have been like an oven. It is one of my vivid childhood memories, and I still feel a guilty pang whenever I remember it.

If parents allow a very young child to have guinea pigs (or any other pets) they must be prepared to take responsibility for them until the

BELOW: *It is too much to expect a child under the age of ten to take full responsibility for the welfare of pets.*

ABOVE: *Children will need help with cage cleaning.*

child is old enough to take over. Too often I have heard Mum or Dad say to their offspring as they carry away my precious babies in a box, "Now you must clean them out and look after them properly." At this stage, the parents get a lecture on their responsibilities before they leave, with a guarantee that, if things do not work out, I will have the guinea pigs back.

It is too much to expect a child under the age of around 10 to take full responsibility for the welfare of pets. There are exceptions: several children spend the day in my shed, helping and wanting to learn.

Cleaning out is hard work for a little one, but feeding is easier, as guinea pigs are little eating machines who will tuck in to offerings enthusiastically. The ideal is for the parents to enjoy the pets with the children, reading books with them and making guinea pig care fun and educational.

One of the biggest hazards of keeping guinea pigs is ignorance of what will stress them and shorten their lives. Here are a few dos and don'ts:

- Do keep an eye on what the children give to the guineas from the garden. Teach them which plants are allowed and which are poisonous (see chapter 3). Use it like a biology lesson. It is wise to give the children only as much information as you think they can take. For instance, recognisable plants such grass, dandelions, clover, and possibly a herb like parsley are enough to start with. Make a firm rule that nothing else may be given. Better safe than sorry.

- Do have the cage on a high table or long legs, out of the reach of small children. They will poke anything green through the mesh, just for the joy of seeing it disappear into the guinea's mouth. Contrary to popular belief, guinea pigs do not always know what is poisonous, especially if they are young, and rely on you to know what is.

- Do protect the guinea pigs from falling from a great height. Make the children sit on the floor when they are having a cuddle. The nearer the ground, the less it will hurt if they suddenly jump. Baby guinea pigs are like little Jack-in-the-boxes – one minute they are sitting quietly and the next, when they think you have relaxed, they will spring out of your hands. You should always be ready

ABOVE: *Guinea pig's tummies are so flat and their legs so short that they are badly winded if they fall.*

for this, and I cannot stress strongly enough that little children should sit on the floor when holding them. When guinea pigs fall from a height, several things could happen:

a. Their front teeth could break as their chin hits the ground. They often pierce the lips at the same time (see chapter 6).

b. Their little tummies are so flat and their legs so short that they are badly winded as they "splat" on to the floor. I have had to administer the kiss of life to several little limp bodies over the years.

After a minute or two and some vigorous rubbing to get the circulation going again they have all survived.

c. The guinea pig could fall on to its back and break its spine. This, of course, is fatal.

d. A leg could break and, while this in itself is not necessarily fatal, it will mean several visits to the vet and almost certainly an anaesthetic. Guinea pigs do not take kindly to prolonged treatment and a lot of pain. They tend to withdraw and give up.

Do teach the children how to hold and catch their pets properly.

ABOVE: *Guinea pigs cannot adjust to sudden changes in temperature.*

Some children are naturals, but most have to be shown. While older children soon learn, younger ones should sit and wait for the guinea pig to be given to them. An adult guinea pig is quite a substantial handful for a child and snuggles into a lap very comfortably. There is a knack to catching a guinea pig who does not want to be caught – which, since the natural instinct of even the tamest guinea is to dash away from danger, is most of the time. The easiest way is to use one hand over the top to pin him down gently, slide the other hand underneath, lifting him up and hold him against your chest. Hold him firmly against you with one hand across his back; support his bottom with your other hand underneath it. If your hand is not big enough to hold him on one hand with the other across his back, you will need to learn another knack. With your hand palm up under his belly and his nose level with your wrist, spread your index finger and middle finger between his back legs either side of the genitals so that the back legs cannot get leverage to jump from your hand.

Don't ever let the children give their own food to their pets. Guineas are herbivores (vegetable eaters), and meat, cheese, chocolate and so on are very bad for them: they might just eat them! I had some sick guineas brought to me that had eaten sausage rolls at a birthday party. It took me weeks to stop their diarrhoea. Don't submit guinea pigs to extreme changes of temperature. Guinea pigs have slow acting body thermometers and cannot adjust to a sudden drop in temperature, which can be fatal to them. Children will want to bring their pets indoors sometimes. This is fine in the summer but can cause problems when winter comes. Homes are heated and, unless you are lucky enough to have your guinea pigs living indoors with you, they are likely to be living in a cold shed. In quite a

ABOVE: *Hold your cavy firmly to your chest.*

ABOVE: *Guinea pigs do not always know what is poisonous especially when they are young, like this baby Swiss.*

ABOVE: *A beautiful Crested English Cream. Remember his instinct is to dash away from danger!*

short time inside a warm house, they will heat up to the point where their ears will feel hot to the touch. Putting them back into a cold shed again could cause pneumonia. The easy way around this problem is for the children to play in the shed in winter, well wrapped up and perhaps with a small safety heater of the kind that cuts out if knocked over. A conservatory would also be ideal, as in winter it is never as hot there as inside the house.

- Don't let children play with guinea pigs in gardens that are not enclosed completely. Please see the chapter on guinea pig accommodation for a description of a garden playpen for children and cavies. An escapee guinea pig is the hardest thing to catch and, if there is only one tiny hole under a hedge or fence, your guinea will find it. Even in an escape-proof garden, a cavy can get into the most unreachable places – under a garden shed, for instance. There he will stay, laughing at your attempts to lure him out, the only possible temptations being food or another guinea pig. You can make a simple cavy trap from two collapsible plastic storage boxes tied together, with lids on them. Put his friend in the first part and some hay and food in the end farthest away from the opening, so that he has to come right in to get it. Leaving one end open, wait and see what happens. He will be able to see and hear the other guinea pig and will not be able to resist the temptation of running up to him. Once he's

in the box, cover the open end quickly. I can guarantee that you will not let him go a second time!

- Don't leave very young children unsupervised with the guinea pigs. They should only be allowed to touch and smooth a guinea in the presence of an adult or much older child. The ability to gauge the difference between holding and squeezing is just not there in a toddler and tiny fingers can do a lot of damage when holding the animal in a vice-like grip, especially if it struggles. Remember that guinea pigs are not toys to keep children happy, but living creatures. We owe it to them to keep them healthy and happy in our care. Children who pick up this caring attitude from their parents will grow up to become responsible pet owners.

Other animals
However kind you think your dog or cat is, never take the risk of leaving your guinea pig running free in the same room. Even if you are there, the unexpected can happen, and often so quickly you would not have time to stop it. When something runs as quickly and suddenly as a small pig, neither cat nor dog could be blamed for obeying its instinct to chase. A heavy paw or sharp claws, even if intended to be friendly or playful, could be fatal. It is no good regretting it afterwards. Guinea pigs are easily stressed and the ordeal even of being confronted by a larger animal that would be a

potential enemy in the wild can be stressful. You may think it is not taking any notice, but its little heart will be beating overtime, pumping the adrenaline ready for flight.

It is also not a good idea to let birds fly over guinea pigs. In their natural habitat, predators often came from the sky in the form of birds of prey, and they still have that inbred fear. In time they would probably get used to them, but I do not think it is fair to put them through that stress.

I do not agree with the practice in some parks and so-called "pet sanctuaries" of having guinea pigs running on the floors of aviaries. Apart from the toxicity of the bird droppings and the mites that can be transferred, the constant fluttering of wings above must be a nightmare to them.

BELOW: *Friends should be supervised.*

ABOVE: *Remember rabbits don't speak cavy – just one reason they shouldn't cohabit.*

Rabbits: It has always been assumed that a rabbit and guinea pig can live together, and some pet shops encourage this to sell their rabbits, as two rabbits rarely get on. In truth this is a very bad alliance, especially for the guinea pig, because:

- Guinea pigs must not eat prepared mixes for rabbits that contain anti-coccidiostat (ACS). Rabbits need this to prevent the disease coccidiosis, but ACS will shorten a guinea pig's lifespan by poisoning its internal organs.

- Guinea pigs are socially-orientated animals

ABOVE: *Rabbits are more restricted in their allowance of vegetable matter – too much makes them scour. Guinea pigs need much more as, like us, they need a daily supply of Vitamin C.*

ABOVE: *Look at the toenails. If they are too long, trim them, and check foot pads for soreness.*

with a special need to bond with their own species. Communication is so important, and rabbits don't speak "cavy." However placid or small they are, rabbits have mad fits of energy now and again during which they kick out with their back legs and dash around the cage. I have seen horrific injuries to spine, ribs and teeth on poor guinea pigs who have not been able to get away from their "friends" in the confines of the hutch.

- Rabbits have a nasty habit of spraying, as anyone who has walked past a hutch at that particular moment will tell you, and their companions are often the target. How would you like to spend your time dodging a shower of very unpleasant smelling liquid? Guinea pigs are very fastidious about their cleanliness, spending much of their time washing themselves like cats, so living under such conditions must be stressful for them.

- Rabbits are more restricted in their allowance of vegetable matter – too much makes them scour. Guinea pigs need much more as, like us, they need a daily supply of Vitamin C.

The only circumstance under which I could tolerate rabbits and guinea pigs together would be in a large run in the garden for a short while – and then only if there was a wooden box upside-down with a doorway only big

ABOVE: *Check whether eyes are crusty or dirty, or whether the head is being held on one side.*

ABOVE: *Hair can be trimmed if it gets too long.*

ABOVE: *Check for scabs around the mouth.*

enough for the guineas to enter it. A cardboard box would not be strong enough, as a rabbit could jump on it, either overturning it or causing it to collapse on the occupant.

Other rodents, Chinchillas, rats, mice, hamsters, gerbils, chipmunks and so on, do not get along with cavies, so never try it to see. A guinea pig role is purely defensive in the wild: it will not attack an enemy – only flee from it. A wild cavy relies entirely on its speed to get away from danger on the many well-trodden paths and trails in the tall grass which is its habitat. It will not turn and fight a predator. Apparently they sometimes play dead when unable to get away, but I have never seen this behaviour in the domestic guinea pig.

Spot Checking

While you are handling and playing with your guinea pigs take the opportunity to check on the following points. Finding a problem early and dealing with it at once is essential for keeping your pets in tip-top condition.

Anus: Check whether hair, hay or any foreign body is visible. Remove immediately.

Bites: These sometimes occur if an argument has occurred between two (usually) good friends – happens to the best of us.

Ears: Check whether they are crusty or dirty, or whether the head is being held on one side.

Eyes: Check whether they are runny or cloudy or have foreign bodies in them.

Feet: Look at the toe nails. If they are too long, trim them, and check foot pads for soreness.

Grease gland: This can become dirty, especially in boars.

Hair: Guinea pig hair can become too long, particularly on long-haired breeds, especially at the back. You can trim this.

Loose droppings: See Diarrhoea.

Lumps: Wherever these are, if they're not part of the normal "design" they shouldn't be there.

ABOVE: *Regular handling alerts the owner to weight changes in their pet.*

Nail Clipping

All guinea pigs will need their nails cut periodically from the age of eight months.

1 White nails are easier to cut as you can see the pink fleshy quick inside the nail. You must not cut too near to this, as it gets pinched.

2 The best way to cut nails is to hold the blades of the clippers horizontally across the nail rather than vertically.

3 Black nails are much harder to cut but, if you look underneath, you will see a groove at the tip.

4 Only cut to where the groove ends and you will not cut too much. If you make the quick bleed, your pet will not bleed to death.

Mouth: Check for scabs at the corners of the mouth or on the lips.

Nose: Check whether it's runny, and make sure both nostrils are clear.

Parasites: Check for wriggly things on the skin or something like dust on the coat.

Skin: There should be no bald patches, redness or scurf.

Teeth: Check that the front teeth are level, and not broken.

Penis: Most important – check that this is not swollen, and remove foreign bodies.

Weight: If you handle them enough you will notice if your cavies seem to lose weight suddenly. This usually means that their food consumption has dropped. Make sure you are giving them enough roughage (hay and dry food) and enough Vitamin C (greens and roots).

Like cats, guinea pigs are meticulously faddy about their appearance.

Spit and Polish (Grooming)

Like cats, guinea pigs are meticulously faddy about their appearance and unhappy when they are dirty, so you can help them with regular grooming. Short-hairs only need a brushing with a pure bristle brush once a week to remove moulting hairs and dirt from the coat.

In addition to weekly grooming, Long-hairs may need a trim around their

ABOVE: *A cheeky Cream.*

back ends to stop the hair from getting wet or soiled. Use a wide-toothed comb for their hair and a fine-toothed comb for under their bellies and between their back legs.

All guinea pigs will need their nails cut periodically from the age of eight months (see page 68). If the worst happens and you make the quick bleed, your pet will not bleed to death. Cavy blood is fast-clotting unless a major vein or artery is cut. Dip the claw into white pepper or hold it under a cold water tap for a few seconds.

All guinea pigs, especially boars, will need the grease gland under the tail stump cleaned at grooming time. The best and safest cleanser is a proprietary emollient (grease dissolver), used by car mechanics for oily hands. Kind to hands and to guinea pig skins, it will soften the hardened grease in about 10 minutes and then just wash off, grease and all.

Shampooing

If I just need to clean the coat I use a combined shampoo and conditioner, but any mild shampoo will do, with your own conditioner used afterwards. Dry with a hairdryer on cool setting.

In Sickness and in Health

Choosing a Vet

Try to find a vet who is good with small animals before you need one. In a group practice there is usually one who specialises in them and is very interested. Others may prefer dealing with larger animals such as cats and dogs while still others, particularly country vets, are happiest in farmyards or stables.

Some veterinary practices put aside special hours during the week for the treatment of small animals, at which time the consultation fee is much less than for cats and dogs, which could represent a considerable saving should your pet require more than one visit. Others charge the same for any animal.

The Cambridge Cavy Trust

Thanks to the Cambridge Cavy Trust and Peter Gurney the days are gone when it was common belief that a sick cavy was a dead cavy. We now have considerable information regarding herbal medicines, and guinea pigs

RIGHT: *Best pet, Audrey.*

Swaddling

When you have to treat, syringe feed or bath your cavy, it is a great help if you can practise the art of swaddling. It takes several goes to get it right but, once it is learned, even the most wriggly animal will succumb to your will. It is not cruel; in fact most of mine seem to enjoy the security of being wrapped up tightly. Some even doze off for a little while.

I use hand towels or, for a small guinea pig, guest towels, while a baby only needs a flannel. Stand Guinea in the middle of the towel, head towards you. Bring the furthest edge behind him over his back, until level with the back of his neck. Fold one side of the towel across and under his chin, making sure his leg is trapped inside. Take it right round until it meets the towel behind his other ear, trapping his other leg. Hold this tight while you repeat the performance with the other loose end of the towel, wrapping this side tightly right around his body. Fold loose-hanging towel under and up. Sit him upright between two cushions and he will stay like this for some time.

seem to respond well to many medicines used by humans – hence their past use in medical laboratories. For this reason, there is now no longer any excuse for an animal to be left to die or to be culled without giving it a chance to live out its normal lifespan.

Under the supervision of Vedra Stanley-Spatcher, the Cambridge Cavy Trust has done the domestic cavy a great service by its research into ailments and remedies, in cooperation with sympathetic vets. Cures are now commonplace where only 20 years ago a poorly guinea pig had little or no chance of survival. Vets were then of little help. It was believed that cavies reacted badly to antibiotics, which meant that the doses prescribed were not sufficiently large to halt the illness, so the cavies died anyway.

You can join the Cambridge Cavy Trust, which is also a cavy hospital, for a small yearly fee, for which you will receive newsletters containing up-to-date information, advice and the opportunity to obtain items for your first aid kit that you should always have to hand. The address and telephone number can be found in Addresses.

Peter Gurney works in close cooperation with Vedra and has produced a book called *Piggy Potions*. This is my favourite cavy reference book. It gives clear, humorous, concise instructions on how to deal with every illness you are likely to come across when keeping cavies. The remedies are simple and easily available, and I shall refer to this book many times in the following text. I have my own favourite remedies, but in *Piggy Potions* there are many alternatives.

Home care – comfort in illness

Before listing the problems that could arise with your guinea pig, I think a few tips on coping with a sick or injured pet would help the process of treating it.

Unfortunately, the first advice given by most books on cavy care is, "Isolate your guinea pig from any others." A cavy is known to become withdrawn and totally depressed when it is unwell or in pain, and for this sociable little animal who, in the wild, would have its family and friends snuggling up to keep it warm suddenly to be all alone will send it into even deeper depression. If the sick one is a sow or boar with its mate, I always leave them together. If it is a mother with her babies, I put another mother sow with her to distract the babies and give her a rest. When an older boar is poorly, the introduction of a younger boar will perk him up and give him an interest in life. There are very few situations necessitating the absolute isolation of a cavy from its companions. If a nasty and highly infectious "bug" has struck, the other cavies will have caught it before any symptoms become apparent. Take the advice of your vet if you have to visit him or her with the sick one.

Such minor ailments as an ear ache or tummy ache could cause a cavy to give up because it is in pain, so the answer is to stop the pain so that he thinks life is worth living

ABOVE: *A sick guinea pig now has a good chance of being successfully treated by the vet.*

again. Children's paracetamol at the dose 0.4ml orally every eight hours, administered by syringe (see Syringe feeding below), can be given to alleviate such pains.

The best pick-me-up for guineas and humans alike is a reputable tonic. A two-week course at the dose of 0.5ml daily for the first week and 0.3ml daily for the second will often give poorly piggies a new lease of life.

ABOVE: *A guinea pig responds to affection.*

A design problem with the guinea pig is that, unlike most animals, it cannot be sick. There is a definite one-way system as far as digestion is concerned: what goes in one end can only come out the other!

Syringe feeding

You must not try to administer any liquid from a syringe or dropper by squirting the whole lot in at once. This would be rather like us having a hose-pipe squirted into our mouths with the tap turned full on! It is better to drip it into the cavy's mouth, a few drops at a time. Liquid is easily inhaled into the lungs and, once there, could set up pneumonia. Guineas cannot easily expel foreign matter from their lungs by coughing and sneezing but, should you see liquid bubbling from the nose, holding the cavy upside-down for a few minutes to allow the force of gravity to help will be beneficial. The cavy will sneeze much of it out before it can do too much damage. I often do this with babies

Treating a Sick Cavy

To syringe feed you will need to cut the barrel of a plastic syringe across and smooth off the sharp edges with sandpaper or an emery board.

The following syringe feeding formula for sick guinea pig is recommended by the CCT:

- **Chinchilla grass pellets (enough to cover the bottom of a cup)**
- **Hot (not quite boiling) water to soak the pellets until they are soft**
- **Mashed potato (an equal amount to the chinchilla pellets)**

Mix the ingredients to a syringeable consistency. The thicker the mix, the smaller the chance of the animal developing diarrhoea.

Most supermarkets do a wonderful range of organic baby food that guinea pigs love. Their favourites are carrot puree and spinach with potato. They enjoy most of the vegetable and fruit recipes in this range, and also the organic carrot juice. If the animal has difficulty in swallowing, these purees are ideal, with a little bran added to thicken them slightly. Offer a few drops of boiled water between mouthfuls of food, and clean the mouth area thoroughly after each feed. Never leave food to dry on the fur around the mouth, as this would attract flies or make the mouth sore.

who have inhaled fluid during the birthing process – it definitely works.

Having perfected your swaddling technique, you can sit your guinea pig up between cushions and feed him in comfort. He will get used to the routine and eagerly look forward to his next meal. Only keep this up until he can eat normally again, or he will become lazy and have you on the run for weeks.

Oldies

As your pet gets older and more infirm there is obviously going to come a time when everything is worn out, and he (or she) will gradually fade. Even so, you can make life as comfortable as possible for your pet by giving extra favourite titbits and extra warmth. Guinea pigs, when dying, are usually very considerate and seem to have a kind of self-hypnotic ability that enables them to shut out the world around them until they just stop breathing.

I am not in favour of having oldies put down unless they are in obvious pain and there is no hope. I do not think they deserve the extreme stress that even their last visit to the vet entails, let alone the pain of a lethal injection. Larger animals, such as cats, dogs and even rabbits, seem to pass away peacefully during the process of euthanasia but, because of their extremely thick, pig-like skin, injections are painful to cavies and they always squeal. If it ever becomes necessary, please ask your vet to use gas or the now old-fashioned ether or chloroform.

BELOW: *An Agouti Cream in peak health.*

Skin Problems

These are the most troublesome problems you are likely to encounter with your pets, which is why I have given them a chapter to themselves.

Mange

There are two types of mange, both of which have several forms, some of which can be transferred to humans, so hygiene is paramount. If you are unfortunate enough to encounter either, always wash your hands after handling your guinea pig.

Sarcoptic mange

This mange, known to breeders as sellnick, is the easier to deal with. It is a parasitic infestation caused by a microscopic mite that burrows under the skin. When humans get this condition (even without being in contact with infected guinea pigs) it is called scabies. In us it is caused by dirt containing the scabies mite getting into a graze or cut or by skin contact with an infected person. In cavies it can be transmitted by the hay, by running on grass or (most usually) by contact with another cavy carrying the mite.

Symptoms: Scratching, biting, restlessness, a very warm body and bare patches where the cavy can reach to scratch and bite. Your usually happy pet will not enjoy being handled and will wriggle and squeal in distress.

Treatment: Two treatments necessary are shampooing and an oral wormer. The

ABOVE: *The coat of a guinea pig with mange.*

shampoos to use are only available through your vet. They are anti-parasitic and anti-fungal, so they will also deal with the fungal form of mange, mycosis. You should shampoo once a month in the summer and every two months in winter as a preventative measure.

The final weapon is a systemic anti-mange treatment. It should contain the active ingredient Ivermectin. Given orally every six months, this will treat your guinea pigs if mange is present and help prevent it if not. The dose is one or two drops (depending on the size of your pet), followed by another dose 10 days later. This must always be combined with shampooing, and not used as a substitute. The shampooing technique is described at the end of the chapter. Your vet should be helpful and administer the treatment for you by placing two drops on the back of the neck of each cavy, which is the method preferred by vets. Otherwise, contact the Cambridge Cavy Trust.

Mycosis

This term covers the whole range of fungal conditions that are used to describe fungal mange in guinea pigs. The form that attacks humans is called ringworm and is easily eliminated by using special anti-fungal cream. I had a patch on my neck a few years ago and traced it back to being licked by a calf's sharp tongue before I could stop him. In guinea pigs it is a much more distressing and difficult problem but regular shampooing will prevent it from occurring. As it is difficult to differentiate between sarcoptic and fungal mange in their early stages the use of shampoo is vital.

Symptoms: Hair loss, and hair around the bald patches that will just come out easily with a gentle tug. The skin is hot to the touch and the cavy will scratch frantically, squeaking in pain. If it is left untreated eventually there will be gritty scurf all over the body with the worst part on the head, around the eyes and under the body. Sometimes fits will occur during the frenzied scratching sessions. Open wounds caused by scratching must be treated with a soothing antiseptic cream, safe for babies' bottoms and for guinea pigs.

ABOVE: *Open wounds can be caused by scratching.*

Treatment: As with Sellnick, the treatment consists of regular shampooing at four-day intervals with treatment shampoo, or you could use an anti-fungal dip. Like the shampoo, this is only available from your vet. It can be made up as a dip with water using 50 parts water to one part dip. Wearing surgical gloves, immerse the cavy on its back, leaving only its nose, mouth and eyes above the water. It is important that the ears are treated too. You can rub around the eyes and mouth with your wet fingers afterwards. It is very important that no part of the body is missed. Leave your cavy to dry naturally in a box containing hay in a warm place.

Lice and mites

The shampoo will also deal with and prevent both of the external parasites that like to make their homes on cavies.

Running lice: Despite their name, these small, lice-like creatures only squirm slowly in the coat. They are brownish in colour and live on the cavy's body, eating skin debris. They cause some discomfort – not as much as the mange mite, but still enough to give rise to scratching and subsequent hair loss.

Static mites: These mites are microscopic and crab-like. Like running lice, they live on skin debris, but travel up and down the hair shaft, shedding their skin as they go and sticking it to the hair with what seems like super-glue, so difficult is it to remove, even with shampooing. The presence of these mites is first apparent by what looks like dust in the coat, but this "dust" cannot be blown away. It looks black on white guinea pigs and white on dark ones. Most fanciers believe that the dust they can see is the mites themselves, but it is actually only their skins visible on the hair. The tiny mites, although not visible, are rummaging around in the cavy's coat.

Anti-mite sprays can be bought from pet shops, and those intended for cage birds are safe for guinea pigs. I use Anti-Mite Spray for Birds. Do not use flea sprays.

ABOVE: *Lice can be detected by parting the coat.*

How to shampoo a guinea pig

Always wear surgical gloves. The shampoo regime is the same for both forms of mange. First use a mild (baby) shampoo to clean the coat. This also removes the grease so that the final wash with the medicated shampoo will penetrate to the skin and do its job.

While washing with the first shampoo, rub hard all over the body to remove all loose hairs, which will be carrying fungal spores on the root. The more of these hairs that are removed, the more successful your treatment will be, even if you are left with an almost-bald guinea pig.

After rinsing off the first shampoo, lather up all over the body with the treatment shampoo, making sure the ears and face get some.

It is important that your guinea pig does not lick the shampoo and, as you have to wait 10-15 minutes before rinsing, this will be an opportunity to use your swaddling technique (see chapter 5). Cradle your pet in your arms (you will both enjoy this) or give it to a child to hold and, when the time is up, rinse off well with warm water.

As with the dip, let the hair dry naturally. Only when doing a cosmetic shampooing should you use a hairdryer.

LEFT: *A plastic washing up bowl makes a good bath.*

6 • A–Z of Guinea Pig Ailments

Abscesses and cysts

Any lumps that appear where they should not be on your pet must be monitored carefully. Some may never grow any bigger. If hard, they are probably fatty cysts, which can be left alone. If they get bigger or grow very fast, then you must go to your vet for advice.

Sometimes you may find that an abscess or boil has grown and burst again before you notice. In this case, the hole it leaves must be washed out with a mild antiseptic solution of antiseptic liquid.

One particularly nasty type of abscess forms under the chin and is called lymphadenitis. This is caused by a hay thistle or other sharp foreign object lodging in the mucous membrane in the throat and needs to be lanced by the vet when it is ready.

Bloat

This condition can cause a painful death, and must be caught quickly. It is caused by your guinea pig eating either mown grass cuttings, which soon heat up and start to ferment, or stale greens. Give your guinea pig grass that has been freshly cut by hand only and make sure its greens are fresh.

Symptoms: A marked and rapid swelling of the belly. The swelling feels hard and balloon-like, not slushy like a half-filled hot water bottle.

Treatment: Act very quickly, giving baby gripe water (at least 2ml) and an indigestion tablet crushed and moistened with water. Repeat in four hours. Meanwhile, try to keep the guinea pig on the move as you would a horse suffering from colic. If your efforts have not begun to take effect after the second dose, go to your vet as an emergency, or death will occur within 24 hours. Tell your vet what you have done. Your prompt treatment will have alleviated the condition and is well worth a try.

Bumble foot

This is a swelling of the pads of the feet, which ulcerates and bursts. This condition often occurs in association with Mycosis, and when this is the cause it must be treated with an anti-fungal preparation. An athlete's foot spray, twice daily, is the easiest but, where there is broken skin or bleeding, dress it with a gauze dressing secured with micropore tape at the top of the leg to make a "sock." Micropore does not stick to the hair – only to itself. Your vet will be able to tell you whether the condition is fungal.

If the condition is not fungal, staphylococcal bacteria are probably the cause. This will need antibiotics. Sometimes a curling toenail cuts into the foot pad and infection sets in. If this is caught early enough, clipping the nails and applying an antiseptic cream will be the only treatment necessary.

Colds

See Ruttling, snuffling and the common cold.

Constipation

Constipation can be recognised by lethargy and the absence of droppings. Give one teaspoon of olive oil once a day and put the guinea pig in a large run or let him run free in

ABOVE: *This Sheltie looks healthy and well cared for.*

a safe place for several hours a day. Increase the intake of fresh food and, if you can find some dandelions and groundsel, these are nature's laxatives for guineas.

Cystitis

This occurs more often in sows than in boars, but the treatment is the same.

Symptoms: The guinea pig will squeak in a series of tiny squeals when passing urine. At the same time, she will lift her rear end slightly and seem oblivious of anything around her for a few seconds until the spasm has passed. She will also be wet underneath. This can be indicative of more serious problems such as bladder stones or severe kidney infection but, if

caught in time, it could be a simple infection.

Treatment: the oldest and most reliable cure, and one widely used for women with cystitis, is barley water, made from pearl barley, and a dose of honey on the end of a teaspoon twice a day. Give as much barley water as the cavy will drink from a syringe or dropper (a drop at a time) until she seems more comfortable. Treat any sore places under the tummy or around the genitals. If there is no change after four days, a visit to the vet will be necessary so that urine tests can be carried out to determine which treatment to prescribe. For further herbal remedies, see *Piggy Potions* by Peter Gurney.

Cysts

See Abscesses and cysts

Recipe for pearl barley water

Make it up in small amounts as it will only keep for 24 hours.

Boil one part pearl barley to eight parts water for 20–30 minutes.
Strain and reserve the water for drinking.
Do not waste the barley, but liquidise it with a little water and your guinea's favourite vegetable.
Add bran to form a crumbly consistency. If your guinea will eat this mash it will be very beneficial.
If you are lucky, she may even take the barley water from a drinking bottle.

Diarrhoea: This can be a serious problem in a cavy and the secret is to catch it at once, so check every day that your pet has a nice, clean bottom.

If the motions are only slightly loose and your guinea is still running around normally and eating with enthusiasm it may be enough to cut down on greenstuff for a few days. Put Vitamin C in the water bottle instead. But if he is looking hunched and miserable, more drastic action is needed. The latest "wonder-cures" are either a liquid anti-diarrhoea treatment, or (even better) "instant" anti-diarrhoea products, which dissolve instantly in the mouth. The guinea pig does not even know he has been dosed. A single treatment may be all that's necessary, or the dose could be repeated after

ABOVE: *Check your guinea's ears for mites.*

twelve hours.

I do not believe in withholding greenstuff completely from a guinea pig with diarrhoea as some experts advise. I have found that tasty green titbits are sometimes the only food a depressed guinea can be tempted with and my sick ones have rallied round sooner if offered them. The only drawback is that, when they are better, they still demand to be pampered, with shrill squeaks. Favourite treats are grass, dandelion (half a leaf), parsley, and, if it is the right season for finding it, Shepherd's Purse is nature's own astringent. If you can find a supply, dry it and keep it for winter use. Guineas shun it when healthy but eat it readily when they have scours.

Finally, it is vital to give plenty of fluids. Rehydration salts in water are the most

effective. Put the preparation into the drinking water, but syringe it in if water is not being taken.

If the diarrhoea persists after treatment, a bacterial infection may be the cause, requiring an antibiotic from your vet.

For other remedies for scours, see *Piggy Potions.*

Ear problems

Should you notice your guinea pig shaking his head and scratching the back of his ear with a back foot, he probably has ear mites. These are little harvest mites transmitted through the hay. Medicated ear drops from your pet shop will soon kill them and regular, thorough cleansing around the curly bits just inside the ear with a damp cotton bud and one drop of the fluid in each ear once a month will keep them at bay.

Never poke anything deeper into the little cavity leading to the inner ear. If there is a foreign body such as a hay seed you could push it further in. If the ear drops do not stop the symptoms after two days, or the cavy holds its head on one side (wry neck), a visit to the vet will be necessary for more detailed examination with an otoscope.

Eye problems

The most common and easily treatable eye problem is a foreign object such as a hay seed, bedding or corn husk in the eye. The first thing you notice is that the eye has lost its brightness and, on close inspection, you will see redness

ABOVE: *Fatty eye*

ABOVE: *Glass eye*

and swelling around the inside of the eyelid and an opaque, bluish look to the pupil. It will look horrendous, and you will be sure that the eye will never look normal again but, within a week of the following treatment, it will be as good as new.

First find the object. I use an eye-dropper and cool, boiled water to flush out the eye, gently pulling the eyelids away from it all the way round, especially in the corners, until I have located the culprit. Nine times out of ten this will be a hay seed. These seeds are like little arrows and go in easily but stick and will not come out again. When you see the point, bear in mind that there is probably a great deal more to follow and work it gently back and forth, slowly pulling outwards at the same time. This method applies if a corn husk has actually

penetrated the eye ball. The trick is, "slow but sure and no messing about." Then I instil a drop of medicated eye drops twice every day to keep the eye moist until all is back to normal.

Sometimes a new mum will roll a wet new baby roughly in the hay while drying it off and the eyes will be poked in the process. This results in one or two sticky, closed eyes, and you will have the job of cleaning them with cotton wool and warm, boiled water. When the crust over a closed eye has softened you will be able to gently prise apart the tiny eyelids and reveal what will look like a dead eye. Pop a medicated eye drop in, and, if the eye gets stuck up again, repeat the procedure until they stay open. You will end up with a perky, bright-eyed minipig in just a few days.

Fatty Eye: This condition causes owners much concern. It is just what it says – a small protrusion of fat around the inside of the eyelid. Sometimes it can only be seen by rolling back the eyelid but, in severe cases, it is plainly visible over the edge of the bottom eyelid, giving the guinea pig a somewhat sulky look. There is absolutely no need to worry about this, as it is an indication that your pet is very well fed, just as gout in humans is attributed to extremely good living. Once fatty eye has developed, nothing can be gained by giving the pig less food – this will only stress him. You could try giving more vegetables and less cereal. This will not help the fatty eye but, if he is obese, it will lengthen his life a little.

Genitals (infection)

Boars: Check the penis regularly. Sometimes debris can prevent the tip of the penis from withdrawing into the sheath, and it will swell and become very sore. It is easy to expel the whole penis and check that it is free of hay, which can wind round and eventually strangle it, causing great pain and permanent damage to the muscle keeping it safely inside. Clean the protruding penis gently with a mild antiseptic solution. For more information see *Piggy Potions*.

Sows: In sows it is possible to find foreign bodies in the vagina or rectum so, if you see the smallest hair or bit of hay protruding, remove it and investigate further.

ABOVE: *Boar genitals*

ABOVE: *Sow genitals*

87

Heatstroke

Caused by exposure to the sun or being kept in an unshaded cage in hot weather. The symptoms of sunstroke include obvious distress, shaking, drooling, laboured breathing. To treat the guinea pig, immediately dunk the legs in cool (not cold) water for 30 seconds. Then wrap the distressed pig in cool, wet towels until it cools down and breathing becomes more normal. A dab of Vick on the nose will open up the bronchial tubes. This is necessary because, since a cavy does not have sweat glands, fluid retention will cause breathing problems. When the panic is over and the cavy is up on its feet and able to drink from the water bottle, fill the bottle up with rehydration fluid. Keep the guinea indoors overnight to avoid night-time chill and pneumonia.

If fluid retention is causing severe breathing difficulties, a trip to the vet will be necessary for a prescription for diuretic tablets.

Impacted rectum

It is nearly always older boars who have this problem, seldom younger ones. It happens because the muscles around the anus become lax and do not expel the soft droppings. These build up into a hard mass and, although the normal droppings can at first pass around it, if left it will block the anal canal.

Treatment: it is very easy to relieve this condition temporarily but, be warned, it is a smelly operation. Wearing disposable surgical gloves, hold the patient on his back in your arms, his bottom over the toilet pan. Smear some petroleum jelly onto the mass and roll back the skin around it gently with your forefinger and thumb. As you ease it outwards slowly the whole mass should drop away, leaving an evil-smelling, white secretion. This should be wiped away with wet cotton wool, and your boar will reward you by hopping around like a spring lamb afterwards in sheer relief. This process may need to be repeated only once a month, but check weekly.

When the problem first occurs it would help if you give the guinea pig two crushed Brewers Yeast tablets weekly for two weeks. This will take the place of the soft droppings, which would normally be taken from the anus and re-ingested. He will gradually adjust by eating more whole grain from the dry food and ingesting more of his normal pellets.

Fungal Mouth and throat infections

Symptoms: Slobbering and difficulty in eating. These are similar to those for overgrown teeth, so check the teeth first.

Treatment: Once overgrown teeth have been discounted, the use of an anti-bacterial oral gel, swabbed around the inside of the mouth twice a day, should get the problem under control. Until the pig has been cured, you will need to syringe feed the patient using the syringe feeding formula for sick guinea pigs described in the "Health and Hygiene" chapter.

Mouth scabs

Symptoms: Crusty sores on the corners of the mouth caused by eating too much acidic food

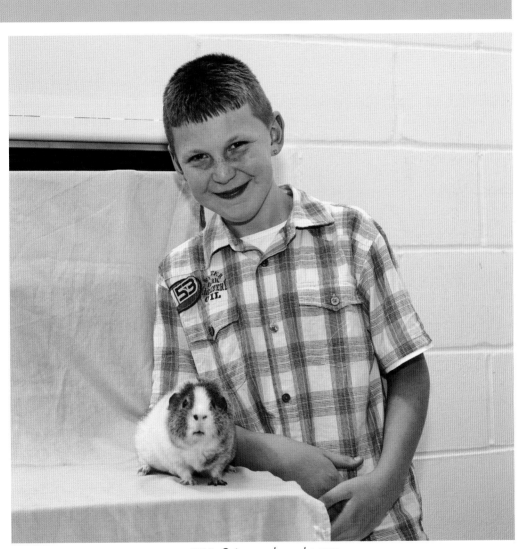

ABOVE: *Guinea and proud owner.*

such as apple, orange or tomato.

Treatment: The old-fashioned cure for thrush in a baby's mouth is Gentian Violet, which is so safe that it can be used on your guinea pig. Dab it on to the scabs with a cotton bud daily, and carry on for a week after the scabs have dropped off. This stains purple, so be careful not to get any on to your hands. Your pet's mouth will be purple, but this soon fades after treatment.

Paralysed back legs

This is nearly always caused by a blow to the spine or pressure on it. Bruising will heal eventually, but nursing will be needed until this happens. Keep the under-belly washed and apply a antiseptic cream to prevent urine scalding until the cavy can lift itself off the floor again, it will get around by pulling itself along by its strong front legs and eating normally until the healing is complete. You can help in the latter stages by exercising its back legs very gently to prevent the muscles from getting lazy.

I have seen this problem several times when a tiny boar has been put in with a huge adult boar without first being bathed to take away the smell of his mother. In his excitement, the big boy will squash the little one. I have also had several pets brought to me in this condition because children have over-hugged their beloved pigs.

Another cause of paralysis is too many vitamins of the D and E type. This is not seen as

LEFT: *Check for post natal sores.*

91

ABOVE: *A judge checks a guinea's teeth.*
RIGHT: *A fine set of whiskers.*

often as it was as fanciers now know the dangers of over-dosing with cod liver oil. Another cause could be lack of Vitamin C (see Scurvy).

In the extremely rare case of the back being broken, the cavy will have to be put down. This will be decided by your vet. I have never had to make the decision, as all my cavies and the others I have seen with paralysed back legs have recovered.

Post natal sores

A guinea pig mum will sometimes pull the hair out from around her under-belly and rump and bite the skin until it bleeds. The easy cure is the soothing camomile cream used by nursing human mothers and completely safe to use on the sow while the babies are suckling.

Ruttling, snuffling and the common cold

Your ears will tell you if your guinea pig has a ruttle. It could be caused by the fact that it is a very short-nosed guinea pig and that, as it gets older, the face shortens and the nasal passage narrows even more. This is a condition for life and need cause you no worry. If it seems very much worse at times, a dab of Vick on the end

of the nose and the front of the paws may help.

Most guinea pig owners do not realise their pets can catch colds and viruses from humans. When you have a cold, don't handle your guinea or its food without washing your hands first and try not to breath on it or sneeze near it. Make sure the children take the same precautions.

If your guinea should catch a cold for any reason, you must keep it warm. Put a cardboard box 60cm x 45cm (24in x 18in) inside a slightly larger one and slip a hot water bottle or heat pad between the walls at one end. At first the guinea will lie near to it if he is cold and, as the bottle cools, he will lie right up against it. Don't forget to fill up again with fairly hot (not boiling) water.

Get out the Vick bottle again to help clear the airways and follow previous instructions. If the lungs sound congested when you hold your ear against the side of the cavy's rib cage (you will hear a clicking sound), give a dose of a medication formulated for nasal congestion, at the dose rate of 0.2ml from a syringe once a day. This is excellent for clearing up mild chest infections in guinea pigs.

If your pet or pets start to look hunched and listless with half-closed eyes and ruffled coats, take them straight off to the vet for some antibiotics.

Scurvy (Lack of Vitamin C)

This complaint is seen only by pet owners who think the dry mix bought from pet shops is a complete food, and don't feed vegetables every day. Some manufacturers are producing

ABOVE: *Fresh greens.*

ABOVE: *Five perky show guinea pigs.*

ABOVE: *Keep a firm hold on your guinea pig!*

mixes with Vitamin C added, and these are the only ones you should use, but fresh vegetables should still be given. If you give them only rabbit mixture with no fresh vegetables, your pets will loose weight rapidly, become very weak and start to lose their hair. Baby vitamin drops must be administered at once at the rate of 0.3ml once a day for two days only and thereafter once a week until recovery is complete. Vitamin C in the water bottle (a small piece of Vitamin C water-soluble tablet) and lots of fresh greens or grass will soon have them back to normal.

Snuffles
See Ruttling, snuffling and the common cold.

Tooth problems
Broken or loose front teeth
If your guinea pig has the bad luck to fall from a height and hit the floor, he nearly always breaks a tooth or teeth and cuts his lip as the tooth pierces it. Sometimes the teeth do not

ABOVE: *An Alpaca*

visibly break off but you find by gently wiggling them that they are loose. In this case, leave well alone. They will soon be lost, but quickly grow again. The guinea pig seems to have a remarkable ability to adapt to a change of eating habits in this situation, and you can help by shredding hard food such as carrot and providing more grass, which is easily transferred to the back molars for munching.

Uneven front teeth

If the front teeth are uneven or one or more are missing you could help by filing the longer ones down with an emery board until the others have grown again. If you really cannot handle the pig firmly enough to do this yourself a visit to the vet will be necessary. However, uneven front teeth can also be a symptom of…

Overgrown back teeth

When a cavy wants to eat but cannot and looks unhappy with life in general, always suspect overgrown back teeth. This can happen when a guinea pig has been off colour for some other reason, after a period of starvation or if not enough munchable food is given in the form of hay, dry food containing biscuit and so on, carrots or beetroot. In this case, investigation by a vet, rodentologist or local breeder will ascertain whether the back teeth are overgrown. If so, they will need to be clipped back so that the guinea pig can resume normal eating. To find the nearest rodentologist in your area, contact the Cambridge Cavy Trust. Clipping the back teeth is an uncomfortable but painless operation. A rodentologist is trained to perform it without anaesthetic but a vet will nearly always anaesthetise, with all the accompanying risks.

Sometimes this problem is genetic and shows itself very early in life, with the back teeth growing over the tongue, trapping it down, or growing outwards into the cheeks. This is found most often in Dalmations and Roans, where interbreeding Dalmatian to Dalmation or Roan to Roan produces malformation of teeth and eyes. Unfortunately, these cavies are very attractive and eagerly sought after by the pet trade. Responsible breeders do not supply them as pets, but some slip through the net. If you should be unlucky enough to get one with this problem as a baby it would be kindest to have it put to sleep, as otherwise it will spend its life with the vet or rodentologist having its back teeth clipped.

Wounds from fighting

These can be quite deep or just a scratch. Superficial ones do not need any treatment other than a dab of diluted antiseptic liquid to cleanse and disinfect. An antiseptic spray can also be used. They soon heal and all you will see is a bald patch or a nick in the ear. The hair will soon grow again and the ear will be a battle scar to be shown off to the guinea pig's friends.

On the more serious side, a wound could become infected, either from the other pig's teeth or from an airborne germ, and form an abscess (see Abscesses).

7 • *Showing Your Guinea Pig*

ABOVE: *These winners are in peak condition.*

Showing cavies can be an interesting and rewarding hobby for all ages. Most weekends there are shows put on by local Cavy Clubs around the Country. Shows vary from the smallest club members shows to large Championship shows. The entry fee is modest, and it is a good way of socialising with like minded people.

With the exception of the pets, cavies are judged to Breed Standard. The standards have been drawn up by enthusiasts over the years, and it is the aim of every breeder to breed a cavy as close to the ideal of the breed standard.

Shows are roughly split into the *Open Classes*, which contain the breeds that have obtained a breed standard: *Rare Variety* section for cavies that have a guide standard, but do not yet have a full breed standard; and *Pets*. Most clubs have sections for Adult and

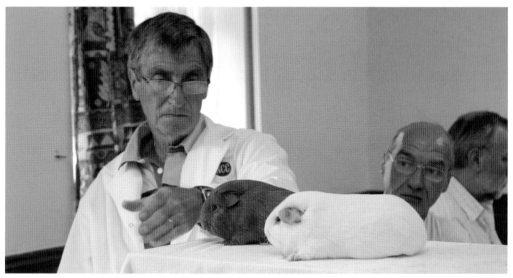

ABOVE: *A judge looking at the profiles of two cavies to determine which will go on to the next section.*

Pen cards and rosettes on a winning pet.

Pets in judging box checking out the competition.

Juvenile exhibitors.

The Open sections consist of the *Self Cavies*, these are smooth coated pigs where colour and shape are the most important factors, and the *Non Self Sections*. The *Non Self* section contains cavies bred for their coat, colour, and markings.

Each breed has its own way of being shown. Self Cavies, and the other smooth coated cavies will need grooming to remove their guard hairs and show the coats off to their best. Rough coated cavies such as the Abyssinian will need to be groomed, but the guard hairs are not removed as this affects the texture of the coat. Rex Cavies must have their guard hairs removed to bring out the best in their coats, but are not bathed as this softens the coat.

Longhaired cavies require much preparation and are not ideal for beginners. Their coats grow an inch a month, and as the cavy gets older, will need to be put into wrappers to

ABOVE: *Plucking out guard hairs.*
RIGHT: *Buff Self Adult*

ABOVE: *Longhaired Merino.*

BELOW: *It is a good idea to consult a specialist in the breed about grooming.*

protect it.

Pets come in all shapes and sizes. They do not have a standard, but are judged on their overall health and wellbeing. They must enjoy being petted and handled.

Whatever their breed, be they pet or purebred, all cavies must be shown clean and free from parasites, cuts and bites, etc.

The grooming and preparation of your cavy before a show will vary, due to the many different coat types, and with this in mind it is a good idea to consult a specialist in the breed concerned for the correct methods. The ideal way to learn about showing is to attend a show, and speak to the people exhibiting, they will be only too happy to speak to you about their chosen breed.

By Julie Gallagher

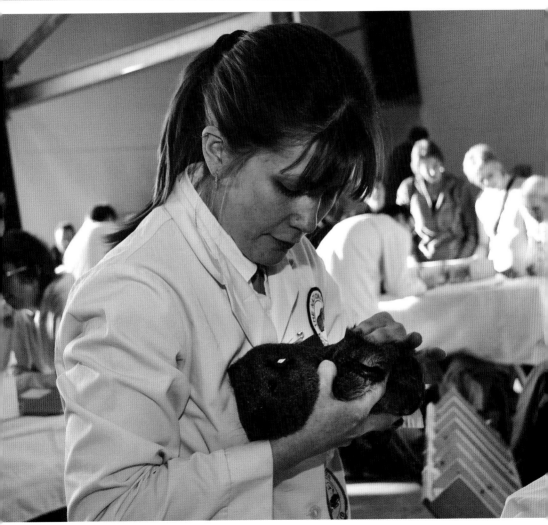

ABOVE: *A judge checks the ticking on an Agouti.*

ABOVE: *The judge looks for good head balance.*

RIGHT: *The judge looks for a good posture.*

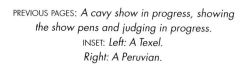

PREVIOUS PAGES: *A cavy show in progress, showing the show pens and judging in progress.*
INSET: *Left: A Texel.*
Right: A Peruvian.

ABOVE: *Judges discussing the finer points.*

ABOVE: *Cavies lined up in a judging box patiently wait to be judged.*

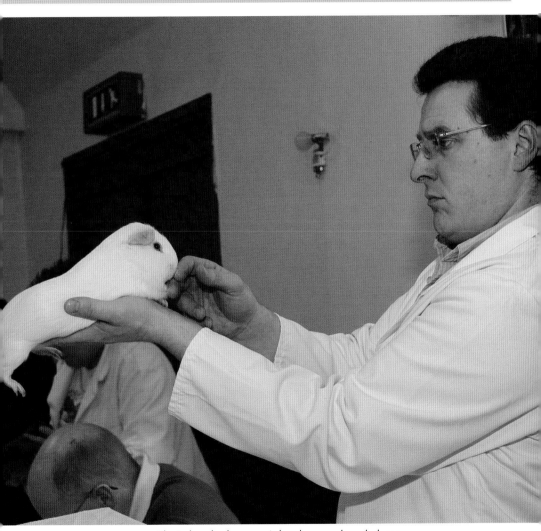

ABOVE: *The judge checks a cavy's head, ear and eye balance.*

LEFT: *Cavies take it easy in the show pens, waiting for judging.*
BELOW: *The judge checks the density of a long haired guinea pig's coat.*

A GUIDE TO WRAPPING

1 Start at the head end of your guinea pig. Have your wraps ready to hand. Position the first wrap at the side of a long section of hair.

2 Now fold up the wrap along the length of your cavy's coat.

3 Secure the wrap with a rubber band to keep the coat in place.

4 Continue the wrapping around the cavy. This shows positioning the wrap on the rear of a long hair.

5 At the back end of your pig, gather the coat together at the rump.

6 Keep the wrap in place while folding.

7 The wrap is folded and ready for the rubber band.

8 The wrap is completed with the rubber band in position.

8 • *Guinea Pig Nursery*

ABOVE: *Nestle and Pillow heavily pregnant.*

I shall only touch briefly on this subject, as this book is intended for those who have pets and may not want to breed babies. In case, like me, you are overtaken by circumstances, here is how it happens.

Mating

A sow will allow a boar to mate with her only for a period of 12 hours every 16 days, and will fight him off as soon as she is pregnant. The sow should be at least six months old and less than a year. Never mate a sow for the first

ABOVE: *Neela pregnant.*

time after she is one year old. By then the pelvic bones will have hardened and fused and she will have great difficulty in delivering, if she can manage it at all.

Pregnancy

The duration of the pregnancy is 68–70 days and, throughout this time, the pregnant sow should be given the best and more of everything nutritious (see chapter 3).

You will be able to see and feel her babies

ABOVE: *Neela giving birth.*

move at about 42 days into pregnancy, when there are about 28 days to go. The babies become more lively as the day draws nearer and the sow begins to look like a beached whale. Do not handle her unnecessarily during the last month.

Birth

She will produce one to six babies, usually while you are not looking! They will probably be clean and dry when you find them. They will be small replicas of their mother and will start eating on the first day. Their eyes will be open

ABOVE: *Neela giving birth.*

ABOVE: *The newborns.*

ABOVE: *Baby Shelties*

and their legs will be strong. Like all herd animals, they must be up and ready to move off with their family soon after they are born.

Separating the sexes

The sow will suckle her babies for three weeks, and then you should separate the baby boars from their mother and sisters. They are capable of mating at this age. You could put them with their father or another adult boar, after rubbing them all over with the litter from the boar's cage. This makes them smell like him rather than like their mother, and will help the bonding process.

If the boar is left with the sow when she has the babies he will perform a post partum mating as soon as the babies are born. This is not a good idea, as feeding one litter while carrying another is too much of a demand upon her reserves.

ABOVE: *Cheeky baby Satin boars.*

Hand rearing

Should you have the misfortune to have to hand rear orphaned babies or "rejects," the best method is to use a teaspoon containing a piece of brown bread soaked in a milk mixture (one part evaporated milk to one part water). The babies will suck on the bread and then sip the milk from the teaspoon. If you put a dish of bread and milk in their cage they will soon transfer to this and feed as and when they want to. I have found that, after a few days, I can get them to drink from a small hamster bottle filled with the milk mixture. They will soon be shouting at you because the bottle is empty.

Warning: Do not let the baby guinea pigs suck from a syringe or dropper. In their eagerness the milk will go into their lungs and pneumonia will set in.

Bottom cleaning

If Mum is not around to do the honours in the bottom cleaning department you will have to do this with the aid of a cotton bud after each feed, as newborn guinea pigs cannot pass urine or motions without this help. The act of gently stimulating the genitals is very rewarding when you actually get results. Once their elimination systems get going (which should only take two or three days) you can leave them to it.

LEFT: *Mother and day old baby Alpaca.*

Growing up

I usually put orphans with another sow, young or old, to keep them warm and teach them how to start eating. The babies eat everything their mother or role model eats and grow very fast. Make sure that you start making extra hutches in time, for I guarantee you will not want to part with your very first litter.

BELOW: *Babies of two litters.*

BREEDS of EXHIBITION CAVIES

written by David R Oulton BVSc MRCVS

9 • *The Breeds and Their Standards of Excellence*

The development of exhibition breeds of cavy is largely shrouded in mystery – in fact it was here one minute as a wild animal and then present in a multitude of varieties and forms the next; what happened between is not well documented and is probably anyone's guess! What is surprising is that so many distinct varieties or breeds have apparently sprung from nowhere over a comparatively short time.

This book details a brief description, pictures and the desired standards of excellence for show cavies of each breed. There are probably quite a few breeds still to be bred and exhibited but their development will be rather less intriguing because hopefully their development will be closely observed and well documented. A self is a cavy that is the same colour all over its body and is smooth coated.

BREEDS CLASSIFICATION

1	self	SELF COLOURS
		(12 standardised)
2	agouti	TICKED VARIETIES
3	solid agouti	
4	argente	
5	dutch	MARKED VARIETIES
6	tortoise and white	
7	himalayan	
8	fox	
9	tan	
10	bicolour	
11	tricolour	
12	tortoiseshell	
13	brindle	
14	dalmation	
15	roan	

16	crested	COATED VARIETIES
17	solid satin	
18	satin non-self	
19	abyssinian	
20	rex	
21	peruvian	COATED LONG
22	alpaca	HAIRED VARIETIES
23	sheltie	
24	coronet	
25	texel	
26	merino	
27	guide standard selfs	RARE VARIETIES
28	gs harlequin	
29	gs magpie	
30	gs belted	
31	gs ridgeback	
32	gs teddy	
33	emerging breeds	

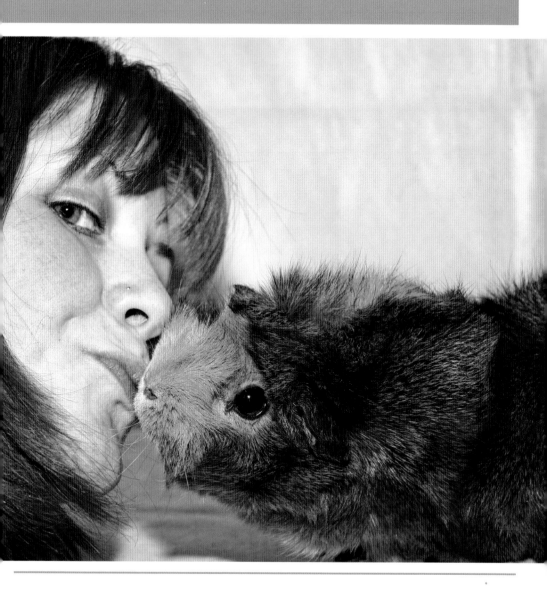

The Self Cavy

BELOW: *Three Black Selfs*

BELOW: *Three Black Selfs*

The self cavy comes in twelve full standard colours: Black, White, Cream, Pink Eyed Golden, Red, Chocolate, Beige, Lilac, Buff, Saffron, Dark Eyed White and Dark Eyed Golden and two further colours have gained guide standards the Slate and the Pink Eyed Cream.

The same standard applies to all colours of self the only differences being those of colour description. Colour is a very important part of the standard, it's important that the top colour that you see fits as closely as possible with the description in the standard, it is important that this top colour is even all over the body and goes right down the hair shafts to the skin. Colour is of course very subjective but the standard tries without being too dogmatic to set

a level playing field.

Texture of coat must be soft and silky, not harsh and course. Self cavies are selected within their breeding programmes to produce this desirable coat. Grooming with particularly the removal of the long guard hairs helps to produce this affect in the show animal.

Type is all important in the show specimen, a broad head and body producing the typical show self cavy. Drooping ears and large bold eyes make the self cavy a very beautiful animal. Over the last century and a half the type of the self cavy has developed out of all recognition from the first cavies imported from South America.

DESIRED STANDARD		Points
Head, Eyes & Ears of which		30
Head	To have a pronounced Roman nose To have good width of muzzle, squared off at the end but rounded at the corners.	
Eyes	To be large, bright, bold and appealing, set wide apart.	
Ears	To be large and drooping, with lower rim parallel to the ground & set with good width between.	
Body Shape	To have short, broad, cobby body with very deep, broad shoulders. To be fit and of good substance, with plenty of firm flesh. To have good size appropriate to age.	25
Colour	Top colour to be lustrous and of glossy sheen, of even shade all over the head & body. Hair on feet to match body colour. Under colour to match top colour down to the skin, giving an appearance free from flakiness. Colours of coat, eyes, ears and pads to match. Descriptions below.	30
Coat	To be soft & silky, clean and short, groomed free of guard hairs.	15
		100

The Self Cavy

pre 1800

1908

1938

1955

2009

DESCRIPTION OF COLOURS

Black	To be deep and lustrous (The black almost has a green tinge). Eyes dark. Ears black. Pads black.
White	To be pure snow white. Eyes pink (P.E.W) or dark (D.E.W.), dark-eyed to be as dark as possible. Ears flesh pink. Pads flesh pink.
Cream	To be a pale cream colour (sometimes described as top of the milk), free from yellow or lemon tinge. Eyes ruby. Pads pink.
Golden	To be a medium gold colour with no suggestion of brassiness, Yellow or red. Eyes pink (P.E.G.) or dark (D.E.G.), dark-eyed to be as dark as possible. Ears pink/golden. Pads pink/golden.
Red	To be a rich, dark colour. Eyes dark. Ears dark. Pads dark.
Chocolate	To be a rich, dark colour. Eyes dark ruby. Ears chocolate. Pads chocolate.
Lilac	To be a medium dove grey colour, with no suggestion of beige. Eyes pink. Ears pink/lilac. Pads pink/lilac.
Beige	To be a medium colour. Eyes pink. Ears pink/beige. Pads pink/beige.
Saffron	To be a medium sand colour (some say the colour of barley straw). Eyes pink. Ears pink. Pads pink.
Buff	To be a deep, rich buff shade with no hint of lemon, apricot or cream. Eyes ruby. Ears pink. Pads pink.

GUIDANCE NOTES

Further description of the self cavy as an aid to judges

The English Self is a solid (single) - coloured cavy bred for Head qualities (head, eyes & ears), Body Shape (particularly shoulders and breadth & compactness of body, Colour and Coat.

The Outline of the English Self cavy should consist of a series of gentle curves, rising from the nostrils to the peak of the shoulders, then dipping to the back and levelling briefly before again dipping over the rear.

Viewed from above the overall impression should be of a brick, rounded at the corners.

Size is very desirable, but not at the expense of cobbyness or quality.

Condition is very important. The cavy should carry plenty of firm flesh but not be gross or flabby.

The sex of the exhibit will usually be apparent from its facial qualities. Boars, if complying with the standard, should not be penalised when in competition with sows on account of slightly different head shape.

Normally the upper weight limit for a 4/5 months Self cavy will be 30 oz or thereabouts. For a cavy of 8 months it will be 37 oz or thereabouts. Although the judge's discretion is absolute as regards whether a cavy is eligible for the class in which it is entered, judges should give careful consideration in cases where these weight limits are exceeded.

SPECIFIC DISQUALIFICATIONS
• Hairs of a different colour according to quantity.
• Areas of darker pigmentation on rims of ears to be penalised.
• White toenails, except on Whites, to be penalised.

BELOW: *Drooping ears and large bold eyes make these Golden Self cavies very beautiful animals.*

The Self Cavy

ABOVE: *Cream Self*

ABOVE: *White Self PE*

ABOVE: *Buff Self*

ABOVE: *SaffronSelf*

The Self Cavy

ABOVE: *Golden Self DE*

ABOVE: *Golden Self PE*

ABOVE: *Black Self*

ABOVE: *Chocolate Self*

135

Agouti

The agouti is a non self ticked variety whose most characteristic feature is its ticking and the distribution of that ticking over the body. The ticking should be prominent, distinct and clean. Intensity and shade of colour are important.

The whole body, except the belly should be evenly ticked. The belly band should be as narrow as possible and distinct from the rest of the body. The feet, chest and head to be evenly ticked and match the rest of the body.

DESIRED STANDARD		Points
Head, Eyes and Ears	Head to be short and broad, with a gently curving profile. Muzzle to be of good width and gently rounded at the nostrils. Eyes to be large, bright and bold and set with good width between. Ears to be large and drooping, with lower rim parallel to the ground & set with good width between.	20
Body Shape	To have short, cobby body with deep, broad shoulders. To be fit and of good substance, with plenty of firm flesh. To have good size appropriate to age.	20
Ticking	To have sharp, level ticking extending evenly over the head, body, chest and feet. Ticking on chest to be carried well down between the front legs. Feet to match body and chest.	30
Colour	Top colour to be bright and lustrous and conform with descriptions below. Undercolour to be carried well down to the skin. Belly colour to be the same colour as the ticking colour but not ticked (to be tipped), even and with well-defined demarcation line; and to be as narrow as possible, although not at the expense of condition.	20
Coat	To be soft & silky, clean and short, groomed free of guard hairs.	10
		100

DESCRIPTION OF COLOURS

Golden	Deep **black** undercolour with dark **golden** ticking. Belly to be a rich mahogany and free from brassiness. Eyes dark. Ears and pads black. Nails to match pad colour.
Silver	Deep **black** undercolour with **silver** ticking. Belly to be a rich silver and free from whiteness. Eyes dark. Ears and pads black. Nails to match pad colour.
Lemon	Deep **black** undercolour with **lemon** ticking. Belly to be lemon. Eyes dark. Ears and pads black. Nails to match pad colour.
Chocolate	Deep rich **chocolate** undercolour with **orange** ticking. Belly to be a rich orange. Eyes ruby. Ears and pads chocolate. Nails to match pad colour.
Cream	Deep rich **chocolate** undercolour with **cream** ticking. Belly to be cream. Eyes ruby. Ears and pads chocolate. Nails to match pad colour.
Cinnamon	Deep rich cinnamon (milk **chocolate** with pinky tinge) undercolour with **silver** ticking. Belly to be a rich silver and free from whiteness. Eyes ruby. Ears and pads cinnamon. Nails to match pad colour.

ABOVE: *Agouti Cream*

137

Agouti

ABOVE: *Agouti Chocolate*

ABOVE: *Agouti Cinnamon*

ABOVE: *Agouti Golden Keisha*

ABOVE: *Agouti Golden Dulcenayer*

Agouti

ABOVE: *Agouti Lemon*

ABOVE: *Agouti Silver*

Solid Agouti

The solid agouti is a relative new comer to the exhibition scene. Essentially the standard is as for the original agouti cavy with the difference that the belly is also ticked. This means that even ticking should be evident on head, back, chest, belly and feet. This new breed experiences problems with ticking on the feet and head but with selective breeding this will improve. The ticking or light fraction of the hair shaft varies but should be short, if too long the cavy will appear very light in colour. The same colours are possible as for the normal agouti.

DESIRED STANDARD		Points
Head, Eyes and Ears	Head to be short and broad, with a gently curving profile. Muzzle to be of good width and gently rounded at the nostrils. Eyes to be large, bright and bold and set with good width between. Ears to be large and drooping, with lower rim parallel to the ground & set with good width between.	20
Body Shape	To have short, cobby body with deep, broad shoulders. To be fit and of good substance, with plenty of firm flesh. To have good size appropriate to age.	20 / 30
Ticking	To have sharp, level ticking extending evenly over the head, body, chest, belly and feet. Feet to match rest of cavy.	
Colour	Top colour to be bright and lustrous and conform with descriptions below. Undercolour to be carried well down to the skin.	20
Coat	Belly colour to be ticked evenly all over, as per the body. To be soft & silky, clean and short, groomed free of guard hairs.	10
		100

Solid Agouti

ABOVE: *Golden Agouti Solid*

ABOVE: *Agouti Solid Silver*

ABOVE: *Agouti Solid Gold*

DESCRIPTION OF COLOURS

Golden	Deep black undercolour with dark golden ticking.
	Eyes dark. Ears and pads black. Nails to match pad colour.
Silver	Deep black undercolour with silver ticking.
	Eyes dark. Ears and pads black. Nails to match pad colour.
Lemon	Deep black undercolour with lemon ticking.
	Eyes dark. Ears and pads black. Nails to match pad colour.
Chocolate	Deep rich chocolate undercolour with orange ticking.
	Eyes ruby. Ears and pads chocolate. Nails to match pad colour.
Cream	Deep rich chocolate undercolour with cream ticking.
	Eyes ruby. Ears and pads chocolate. Nails to match pad colour.
Cinnamon	Deep rich cinnamon (milk chocolate with pinky tinge) undercolour with silver ticking.
	Eyes ruby. Ears and pads cinnamon. Nails to match pad colour.

Argente

ABOVE: *Argente Lilac*

DESCRIPTION OF COLOURS

Golden/Lilac	Eyes pink. Ears pink/lilac. Pads pink. Deep lilac undercolour with golden ticking. Belly to be golden.
Golden/Beige	Eyes pink. Ears pink/beige. Pads pink. Deep beige undercolour with golden ticking. Belly to be golden.
Lemon/Lilac	Eyes pink. Ears pink/lilac. Pads pink. Deep lilac undercolour with lemon ticking. Belly to be lemon.
Lemon/Beige	Eyes pink. Ears pink/beige. Pads pink. Deep beige undercolour with lemon ticking. Belly to be lemon
White/Lilac	Eyes pink. Ears pink/lilac. Pads pink. Deep lilac undercolour with white ticking. Belly to be white.
White/Beige	Eyes pink. Ears pink/beige. Pads pink. Deep beige undercolour with white ticking. Belly to be white.

ABOVE: *Argente Golden*

ABOVE: *Argente Cream*

Argente

The Argente is a Ticked Cavy with each hair shaft being two colours. The Argente is a pink-eyed ticked cavy in which the ticking covers the whole of the body other than the belly. When judging Argentes, the emphasis is on quality of ticking, colour, type and condition. They come in the following recognised colours: Gold/Lilac, Gold/Beige, White/Lilac, White/Beige, Cream/Lilac and Cream/Beige. The Argente is genetically a pink-eyed Agouti. In 2009 the Argente does not have its own specialist club of fanciers and is catered for by the Rare Varieties Cavy Club.

DESIRED STANDARD		Points
Head, Eyes and Ears	Head to be short and broad, with a gently curving profile. Muzzle to be of good width and rounded at the nostrils. Eyes to be large, bright and bold and set with good width between. Ears to be large and drooping, with lower rim parallel to the ground & set with good width between.	20
Body Shape	To have short, cobby body with deep, broad shoulders. To be fit and of good substance, with plenty of firm flesh. To have good size appropriate to age.	20
Coat Appearance	Throughout the head, body, chest and feet the Argente should have individual hairs ticked with gold, lemon or white over a base colour of beige or lilac. This should produce a shimmering, 'shot silk' effect that is even all over the body, including around the eyes and on the chest and feet.	30
Colour	Top colour to be bright and lustrous and conform with descriptions below. Belly colour to be the same colour as the ticking colour but not ticked (to be tipped), even and with well-defined demarcation line; and to be as narrow as possible, although not at the expense of condition.	20
Coat	To be soft & silky, clean and short, groomed free of guard hairs.	10
		100

Dutch

The Dutch cavy is a marked variety and appears at shows in the non self section. The majority of points in the standard are allocated for its markings which give a very attractive animal. A very specific pattern is detailed in the standard for these markings which above all must give a balanced appearance. This cannot be overemphasised as faults are very common with either the cheeks, saddle or stops but their balanced appearance is of paramount importance. Dutch come in the following colours: Red, Black, Chocolate, Cream, Lilac, and in five agouti colours (Golden, Chocolate, Silver, Cinnamon and Cream).

Dutch Black

Dutch

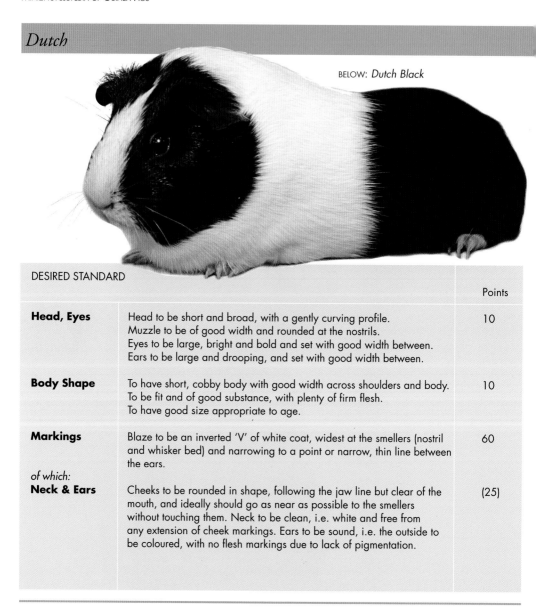

BELOW: *Dutch Black*

DESIRED STANDARD

		Points
Head, Eyes	Head to be short and broad, with a gently curving profile. Muzzle to be of good width and rounded at the nostrils. Eyes to be large, bright and bold and set with good width between. Ears to be large and drooping, and set with good width between.	10
Body Shape	To have short, cobby body with good width across shoulders and body. To be fit and of good substance, with plenty of firm flesh. To have good size appropriate to age.	10
Markings	Blaze to be an inverted 'V' of white coat, widest at the smellers (nostril and whisker bed) and narrowing to a point or narrow, thin line between the ears.	60
of which: **Neck & Ears**	Cheeks to be rounded in shape, following the jaw line but clear of the mouth, and ideally should go as near as possible to the smellers without touching them. Neck to be clean, i.e. white and free from any extension of cheek markings. Ears to be sound, i.e. the outside to be coloured, with no flesh markings due to lack of pigmentation.	(25)

LEFT: *Dutch Chocolate*

		Points
Saddle & Undercut	Saddle and undercut to be positioned midway between the neck and hips; to be cut as a straight line with the sides at right angles to the body. A higher cut (i.e. cut line nearer to the head) is preferable to a low, 'slipping' one (i.e. further back towards the hips).	(20)
Foot Stops	There must be two foot stops and these should be of the same length ('balanced'), ideally being cut midway between the hock and the toe ends. Each stop must have three white toenails, and the white pigmentation on the pad must not run to the hock. The hairs covering the toes must be white.	(15)
Colour	Colours ideally to conform as nearly as possible to ESCC or NACC Standards, although slight variations from these should not be penalised so long as colour is rich, even, of glossy sheen, free from hairs of a different colour (brindling, roaning, or any patches), with the colour carried well down to the skin to avoid any appearance of flakiness. To be appropriate to breed colour.	15
Coat	To be soft, clean and groomed free of guard hairs.	5
		100

Dutch

ABOVE: *Dutch Red*

DESCRIPTION OF COLOURS

Golden/Lilac	Eyes pink. Ears pink/lilac. Pads pink. Deep lilac undercolour with golden ticking. Belly to be golden.
Golden/Beige	Eyes pink. Ears pink/beige. Pads pink. Deep beige undercolour with golden ticking. Belly to be golden.
Lemon/Lilac	Eyes pink. Ears pink/lilac. Pads pink. Deep lilac undercolour with lemon ticking. Belly to be lemon.
Lemon/Beige	Eyes pink. Ears pink/beige. Pads pink. Deep beige undercolour with lemon ticking. Belly to be lemon
White/Lilac	Eyes pink. Ears pink/lilac. Pads pink. Deep lilac undercolour with white ticking. Belly to be white.
White/Beige	Eyes pink. Ears pink/beige. Pads pink. Deep beige undercolour with white ticking. Belly to be white.

ABOVE: *Dutch Cream*

ABOVE: *Dutch Chocolate*

Tortoise and White

ABOVE: *A judge considers the merits of these tortoise and white cavies.*

ABOVE: *A tortoise and white cavy showing his belly markings.*

The tortoise and white cavy is a smooth coated non self breed. This is a very popular and attractive breed. This is a breed for the sportsman because the gamble of producing one near the standard is very much a matter of luck, though years of dedication to line and clean patches free from brindling must play a major part in producing these highly attractive but often exasperating cavies. The ideal is a

DESIRED STANDARD		Points
Head, Eyes and Ears	Head to be short and broad, with a gentle curving profile. Muzzle to be of good width and rounded at the nostrils. Eyes to be large bright and bold and set with good width between. Ears to be large and patches to be placed on each, drooping, and set with good width between.	10
Body Shape	To have a short cobby body with good width across shoulders and body. To be fit and of good substance, with plenty of firm flesh. To have good size appropriate to age.	10
Markings	To consist of square cut patches of black, red and white colour, of uniform shape and evenly distributed on each side of the body on either side of a central line formed by the meeting of patches of different colours	60
of which: **Head Markings**	Head ideally to have two colours divided down the centre. A different colour on each side of the head divided by a blaze of a third colour is almost as desirable.	(5)
Line and Distribution of Patches	Patches to be placed on each side of the body so as to give no overlaps on the central line top and under. Each side of the body of the cavy to have three or more patches. Each side of the cavy to have patches of all three colours.	(30)
Shape and Clarity of Patches	Patches to be square cut with straight edges and of equal size. Patches to be clean cut and distinct from each other, and with no intermingling of colours.	(25)
Colour	Colours to be rich, even and of glossy sheen and carried well down to the skin to avoid any appearance of flakiness, with patches free from hairs of a different colour (brindling and roaning). Black to be jet black. Red to be rich, maybe lighter than the ESCC red but must not be pale or washed out. White to be pure and clean. Eye colour to be dark, but a blue tinge (when the head has a white patch) is not a fault.	15
Coat	To be soft, clean and groomed free of guard hairs.	5
		100

Tortoise and White

SPECIFIC FAULTS

Line Faults	
Band	A patch of colour going all the way around the body.
Belt	A patch of colour going more than half way round the body.
Overlap	A patch of colour overlapping the centre line, top or under.
Solid Head	Head of a single colour.
Dutch-pattern Head	Head with the same colour on each side of the head with a blaze of a different colour.

DISTRIBUTION FAULTS

Missing Colour	An absence of any of the three colours on either side of the cavy.
Shortage of Patches	Less than three patches on any side of the body, two patches being better than one.
Clarity Faults	An absence of any of the three colours on either side of the cavy.
Brindling / Roaning:	Intermixing of any colours (white for roaning) where patches meet.
Colour Faults	(To be penalised according to extent of failing)
Brindling / Roaning:	Intermixing of hairs of a different colour (white for roaning) within patches. A small amount of brindling or roaning should not be too harshly penalised on an otherwise well-marked exhibit. Some young cavies may show evidence of roaning that will disappear with the adult coat.

bright dazzling animal displaying its three colours of red, black and white brilliantly contrasting in squares or patches up one side and down the other in a different colour sequence. The chequerboard pattern of square cut patches of approximately equal size produces a dividing line formed by the meeting of colours on opposite sides of the body. Ideally no patches should overlap the central line, either on top or under. There is no correct sequence of patches, but in considering the overall quality of the breed the balance of patches and colour on each side and top and under is important. On well marked exhibits four or five patches on each side would be preferable to three, but not at the expense of a loss of uniformity in size and shape of patches. Each patch should consist of a solid colour, clearly defined from surrounding patches, and with no intermingling of hairs of different colours. When a judge assesses a tortoise and white on the show bench the quality of markings is by far the most important aspect of the cavy, minor faults in type, head shape and ear carriage are of little importance.

ABOVE: *Tortoise and white, showing the head divide.*

Himalayan

The Himalayan is a non self variety of cavy whose most characteristic feature is its markings and their distribution around the cavy's body. In fact the Himalayan is an albino cavy that develops pigment on its nose, ears, and feet (we call these the points) during the first few months of its life. The points or markings should be prominent, distinct and

DESIRED STANDARD		Points
Head, Eyes	Head to be short and broad, with a gently curving profile. Muzzle to be of good width and rounded at the nostrils. Eyes to be large, bright and bold and set with good width between. Ears to be large and drooping, and set with good width between.	10
Body Shape	To have short, cobby body with good width across shoulders and body. To be fit and of good substance, with plenty of firm flesh. To have good size appropriate to age.	10
Markings (Points) *of which:*	To consist of even, sharply defined dark points on face, ears and feet with clear demarcation from the background white body colour.	50
Smut	To be prominent, wider at the nostril end, ideally pear-shaped and carried well between the eyes; sharply defined and intensely coloured black or rich milk chocolate.	(25)
Ears	To be intensely coloured black or rich milk chocolate, dense to the base.	(5)
Feet	To be even and intensely coloured black or rich milk chocolate; sharply defined, with colour carried well up the legs and including nails and pads.	(20)
Colour (of body)	To be pure white and as free from body pigment (stain) as possible.	25
Coat	To be soft, clean and groomed free of guard hairs.	5
		100

ABOVE: *Black Himalayan*

ABOVE: *Chocolate Himalayan*

Himalayan

DESCRIPTION OF COLOURS

Himalayans may be exhibited in two colours:
Black Himalayan to have black pads.
Chocolate Himalayan to have dark pink to chocolate pads.
Jet black and rich milk chocolate are the desired shades.
Both colours of Himalayan should have bright red eyes.

Specific Disqualifications
White patches in markings.
Unpigmented areas in foot pads.
Unpigmented toenails.

Specific Faults
Uneven markings, speckled with white hairs giving a 'peppered' effect.
Poor demarcation between Points and body colour.

PREVIOUS PAGES: *Himalayan Black*

RIGHT: *Himalayan Chocolate*

clean. Intensity and shade of colour in these points is very important. The contrast between the sharpness of these points and the desirable pure white body colour is the essence of this breeds appeal. Sharpness and contrast are the most important points in the makeup of a good Himalayan cavy. Judges are asked to not excessively penalise young Himalayans for white hairs on the points which will moult out with age. Even young adults will still retain some white hairs on the inside of the ears. In very cold weather the pure white body colour gains some pigment. In hot weather in the summer the intense colour of the feet and smut fades somewhat.

Fox

The Fox is a smooth coated non self cavy breed, essentially a solid coloured cavy with specified fox/white markings. These fox/white markings are around the face (eye circles, pea spots, and nostril and jowl areas) chest and belly, thickly laced with white- tipped ticking on the sides. The belly colour is carried down onto the inside of each leg. The marking should be prominent, distinct and clean. Intensity and shade of colours is important. A Fox shall have very good and well distributed markings to be considered a good representative of the breed.

ABOVE: *Black Fox*

ABOVE: *Lilac Fox*

Fox

DESIRED STANDARD		Points
Head, Eyes	Head to be short and broad, with a gently curving profile. Muzzle to be of good width and rounded at the nostrils. Eyes to be large, bright and bold and set with good width between. Ears to be large and drooping, and set with good width between.	10
Body Shape	To have short, cobby body with good width across shoulders and body. To be fit and of good substance, with plenty of firm flesh. To have good size appropriate to age.	10
Markings	To have solid base colour all over body except for white areas that must be solid, clearly defined and distinct, both from the base colour and each other.	50
Nostrils, Jowls, Chest & Throat	Nostril area, jowls and chest to be white. There should be a clear band of base colour across the throat.	(15)
Eye Circles, Pea-Spots	White eye circles to be clearly distinguishable. On the forehead beside each ear should be clear white markings, known as pea spots. Should not run in to the ears.	(15)
Belly, Legs	Belly to be white, with minimal darker under colour showing and with belly colour only just visible when viewed from the side. The inside of each leg should be white, with base colour on the outside.	(10)
Sides	Sides, including sides of hips, to be thickly laced with long white-tipped ticking.	(10)

LEFT: *Tan Slate Fox*

		Points
Colour	Base colour to conform to ESCC requirements, be even, with glossy sheen and carried down to the skin. White to be pure and clean, Eye colour to match requirements of relevant ESCC base colour. Toenail pigmentation to match ESCC requirements appropriate to toe colour.	25
Coat	To be soft, clean and groomed free of guard hairs, other than on flanks where grooming may remove the desirable white markings.	5
		100

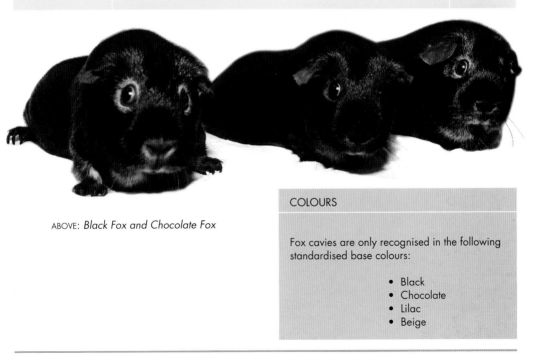

ABOVE: *Black Fox and Chocolate Fox*

COLOURS

Fox cavies are only recognised in the following standardised base colours:

- Black
- Chocolate
- Lilac
- Beige

Tan

The Tan is a smooth coated non self cavy breed, essentially a solid coloured cavy with specified tan markings. These tan markings are around the face (eye circles, pea spots, and nostril and jowl areas) chest and belly, thickly laced with tan- tipped ticking on the sides. The belly colour is carried down onto the inside of each leg. The markings should be prominent, distinct and clean. Intensity and shade of colours is important. A Tan shall have very good and well distributed markings to be considered a good representative of the breed.

COLOURS

Tan cavies are only recognised in the following standardised base colours:

- Black
- Chocolate
- Lilac
- Beige

BELOW: *Tan Beige*

ABOVE: *Tan Black*

ABOVE: *Tan Lilac*

Tan

DESIRED STANDARD		Points
Head, Eyes	Head to be short and broad, with a gently curving profile. Muzzle to be of good width and rounded at the nostrils. Eyes to be large, bright and bold and set with good width between. Ears to be large and drooping, and set with good width between.	10
Body Shape	To have short, cobby body with good width across shoulders and body. To be fit and of good substance, with plenty of firm flesh. To have good size appropriate to age.	10
Markings	To have solid base colour all over body except for tan areas that must be solid, clearly defined and distinct, both from the base colour and each other.	50
Nostrils, Jowls, Chest & Throat	Nostril area, jowls and chest to be tan. There should be a clear band of base colour across the throat.	(15)
Eye Circles, Pea-Spots	Tan eye circles to be clearly distinguishable. On the forehead beside each ear should be clear tan markings, known as pea spots. Should not run in to the ears.	(15)
Belly, Legs	Belly to be tan, with minimal darker under colour showing and with belly colour only just visible when viewed from the side. The inside of each leg should be tan, with base colour on the outside.	(10)
Sides	Sides, including sides of hips, to be thickly laced with long tan tipped ticking.	(10)

ABOVE: *Tan Chocolate*

		Points
Colour	Base colour to conform to ESCC requirements, be even, with glossy sheen and carried down to the skin. Tan to be pure and clean, Eye colour to match requirements of relevant ESCC base colour. Toenail pigmentation to match ESCC requirements appropriate to toe colour.	25
Coat	To be soft, clean and groomed free of guard hairs, other than on flanks where grooming may remove the desirable tan markings.	5
		100

Tan

ABOVE: *Tan Slate Nat Fox*

RIGHT: *Tan Slate*

Bicolour

ABOVE, AND FOLLOWING TWO PAGES: *Bicolour*

Two coloured smooth coated cavies marked with alternate coloured patches either side of mid line stretching from back to front mid back and mid belly. Bicolours may be two colours of any recognised self or agouti colour. Each patch should consist of a solid colour, clearly defined from surrounding patches, and with no intermingling of hairs of a different colour.

The tortoiseshell is a bicolour made up of black and red and is one of the country's oldest recognised breeds but has always been very rare.

DESIRED STANDARD		Points
Head, Eyes and Ears	Head to be short and broad, with a gently curving profile. Eyes to be large, bright and bold and set with good width between. Ears to be large and drooping, and set with good width between.	10
Body Shape	To have short, cobby body with good width across shoulders and body. To have good size appropriate to age.	10
Markings *of which:*	To consist of patches of any two colours other than black and red together evenly distributed on each side of the body on either side of a central line formed by the meeting of patches of different colours.	60
Head Markings	Head to have two colours divided down the centre.	(5)
Line & Distribution of Patches	Patches to be placed on each side of the body so as to give no overlaps over the central line top or under. Each side of the body of the cavy to have three or more patches.	(30)
Shape & Clarity of Patches	Patches to be square-cut with straight edges and of equal size. Patches to be clean-cut and distinct from each other, with no intermingling of colours.	(25)
Colour	Colours to conform as nearly as possible to ESCC (Self colours), NACC (Agouti colours) or RVCC (Argente colours) Standards, although slight variations from these should not be penalised so long as colour is rich, even, of glossy sheen and carried well down to the skin to avoid any appearance of flakiness.	15
	Eye colour to be dark or pink, as appropriate to the constituent colours.	5
Coat	To be soft, clean and groomed free of guard hairs.	
		100

Bicolour

Tricolour

DESIRED STANDARD		Points
Head, Eyes and Ears	Head to be short and broad, with a gently curving profile. Muzzle to be of good width and rounded at the nostrils. Eyes to be large, bright and bold and set with good width between. Ears to be large and drooping, and set with good width between.	10
Body Shape	To have short, cobby body with good width across shoulders and body. To be fit and of good substance, with plenty of firm flesh. To have good size appropriate to age.	10
Markings	To consist of square cut patches of white and any two other colours other than black and red together, of uniform shape and evenly distributed on each side of the body on either side of a central line formed by the meeting of patches of different colours.	60
Head Markings	Head ideally to have two colours divided down the centre. A different colour on each side of the head divided by a blaze of the third colour is almost as desirable.	(5)
Line & Distribution of Patches	Patches to be placed on each side of the body so as to give no overlaps over the central line top or under. Each side of the body of the cavy to have three or more patches. Each side of the cavy to have patches of all three colours.	(30)
Shape & Clarity of Patches	Patches to be square-cut with straight edges and of equal size. Patches to be clean-cut and distinct from each other, with no intermingling of colours.	(25)
Colour	Colours to conform as nearly as possible to ESCC (Self colours), NACC (Agouti colours) or RVCC (Argente colours) Standards, although slight variations from these should not be penalised so long as colour is rich, even, of glossy sheen and carried well down to the skin to avoid any appearance of flakiness.	15
	Eye colour to be dark or pink, as appropriate to the constituent colours.	5
Coat	To be soft, clean and groomed free of guard hairs	
		100

COLOURS

Tricolours may be shown in white plus any two fully standardised colours as recognised by the ESCC, NACC, or RVCC, with the exception of red, black and white, this being the Tort & White, and D.E. golden, black and white, which is insufficiently differentiated in colour from the Tort & White.

ABOVE: *Tricolour*

The Tricolour is a marked variety which is essentially a patched cavy of three distinct colours. These colours can be one of the colours defined for self cavies or can be one of the agouti colours. The important characteristic of the breed is that the patches are evenly distributed around the body and of as uniform size as possible, the cavy will also have a line along the backbone and centre of belly meeting nose and "tail" separating the different coloured patches.

GUIDANCE NOTES

The Tricolour is a smooth coated cavy, carrying a chequerboard pattern of square- cut patches of three colours, one being white, of equal size, with a dividing line formed by the meeting of patches on opposite sides of the body running the length of the cavy both top and underside. No patches should overlap the central line, either on top or under side.

There is no set sequence for the patches; but in considering the quality of a Tricolour the overall balance of patches and colour on each side and top & under is important. On well marked exhibits four or five patches

on each side would be preferable to three, but not at the expense of a loss of uniformity in the size and shape of the patches. Each patch should consist of a solid colour, clearly defined from surrounding patches, and with no intermingling of hairs of a different colour. Because a fault that is seen readily on the top side of the cavy has a greater adverse impact on the overall appearance than one which is 'hidden' underneath, preference should be given to a cavy with a good top and less good under than one with the opposite characteristics. However,

patching on the belly must be taken into account when considering overall quality. When assessing the Tricolour, the quality of the markings is by far the most important aspect of the cavy, and minor faults in type, such as a straight head or ears not drooping, are of very little significance. However, soundness of all of the three colours is important to creating the overall impact of the patchwork. Because it is extremely difficult to fix the desired markings on the Tricolour, judges should not be too harsh in assessing 'good attempts' with clear patches and solid colour.

175

Tortoiseshell

The tortoiseshell cavy is a smooth coated variety with a patchwork pattern of red and black squares or oblongs. The patches as far as possible should be of uniform size and uniform shape and should be so positioned to give a distinct dividing line running in the centre of the back from nose to "tail" and again in a likewise manner on the belly. As with all varieties balance is important, there is no set order for the patches or set pattern, it is fairly important to avoid overlapping the central line or to avoid patches running along the sides of the body so reducing the balance of the patches. Another common fault is brindling or mixing of the red and black hairs, this easily increases in a breeding programme and should be avoided as much as possible.

This is a very difficult and a very old breed. The breed has never been very popular but has always existed in low numbers. Judges quite rightly accept minor faults in type etc. and give credit to good attempts at clear balanced patchwork.

ABOVE: *Tortoiseshell*

DESIRED STANDARD		Points
Head, Eyes and Ears	Head to be short and broad, with a gently curving profile. Muzzle to be of good width and rounded at the nostrils. Eyes to be large, bright and bold and set with good width between. Ears to be large and drooping, and set with good width between.	10
Body Shape	To have short, cobby body with good width across shoulders and body. To be fit and of good substance, with plenty of firm flesh. To have good size appropriate to age.	10
Markings	To consist of patches of black and red, evenly distributed on each side of the body on either side of a central line formed by the meeting of patches of different colours.	60
Head Markings	Head to have two colours divided down the centre.	(5)
Line & Distribution	Patches to be placed on each side of the body so as to give no overlaps over the central line top or under of patches. Each side of the body of the cavy to have three or more patches.	(30)
Shape & Clarity	Patches to be square-cut with straight edges and of equal size.	(25)
Colour	Colours ideally to conform as nearly as possible to ESCC Standards, although slight variations from these should not be penalised so long as colour is rich, even, of glossy sheen and carried well down to the skin to avoid any appearance of flakiness. To be free from white hairs (see Faults below). Eye colour to be dark.	15
Coat	To be soft & silky, clean and short, groomed free of guard hairs.	5
		100

Brindle

ABOVE: *The more common Abyssinian Brindle*

The Brindle is a smooth cavy with the red and black hairs intermingled – a red and black salt and pepper like effect. The evenness of the intermingling and the richness of the red hairs determines how striking the effect is. It is very difficult to get a perfect mix of these two hair colours, patches of varying size are often present. It is far more common to see the brindle as a colour of Abyssinian but this is a completely different breed of cavy. Type, ears, eyes, size and shape are as for self cavies.

GUIDANCE NOTES

The Brindle cavy has red and black hairs intermingled all over the body, including the head and feet. Brindles may be 'dark' (where there is an excess of black hairs over red), 'light', where there is an excess of red hairs over black, or 'medium', where the black and red hairs are present in equal quantities.

The ideal colour effect is medium, but evenness of brindling is far more important than the exact shade produced, so long as the darkness or lightness are not excessive.

178

DESIRED STANDARD		Points
Head, Eyes and Ears	Head to be short and broad, with a gently curving profile. Muzzle to be of good width and rounded at the nostrils. Eyes to be large, bright and bold and set with good width between. Ears to be large and drooping, with lower rim parallel to the ground & set with good width between.	10
Body Shape	To have short, cobby body with deep, broad shoulders To be fit and of good substance, with plenty of firm flesh. To have good size appropriate to age.	10
Markings	To consist of an even intermixing of red and black hairs all over the body. Black and red hairs should be in equal proportions, with no areas of distinct black or red colouration.	60
of which:		
	HEAD	(10)
	FEET	(10)
	BODY	(30)
	BELLY	(10)
Colour	Colours ideally to conform as nearly as possible to ESCC Standards, although slight variations from these should not be penalised so long as colour is rich, even, of glossy sheen and carried well down to the skin to avoid any appearance of flakiness. Eye colour to be dark.	15
Coat	To be soft & silky, clean and short, groomed free of guard hairs.	5
		100

Dalmation

The Dalmation is a white guinea pig with coloured marking similar to those of the dog from which its name originates. In the UK the name is spelt with an 'o' but in USA and Australia it is spelt in the same way as the dog, Dalmatian.

The first Dalmation appeared as a mutation from Self Black guinea pigs in the UK in the 1970s. They have since been developed into a very attractive breed with solid coloured cheeks divided by a white blaze on the head, solid coloured feet and distinct spotting on the body. They are now accepted in all the recognised colours including Agouti and Argente. Whilst perfect show specimens are difficult to achieve any 'near misses' make very pretty pets.

Care must be taken when breeding this variety. If two Dalmations are mated together there is a 25% possibility of a malformed baby. These babies are pure white and blind. They are sometimes referred to as 'micropthalmic' or 'lethal whites'. Although the latter term is

COLOURS

Tricolours may be shown in white plus any two fully standardised colours as recognised by the ESCC, NACC, or RVCC, with the exception of red, black and white, this being the Tort & White, and D.E. golden, black and white, which is insufficiently differentiated in colour from the Tort & White.

ABOVE: *Dalmation Black*
NEXT PAGES: *Dalmation Chocolate*

DESIRED STANDARD		Points
Head, Eyes and Ears	Head to be short and broad, with a gently curving profile. Muzzle to be of good width and rounded at the nostrils. Eyes to be large, bright and bold and set with good width between. Ears to be large and drooping & set with good width between.	10
Body Shape	To have short, cobby body with deep, broad shoulders To be fit and of good substance, with plenty of firm flesh. To have good size appropriate to age.	10
Markings *of which:*		60
Head Markings	To have a white blaze with solid colour on either side, giving a well balanced appearance.	(20)
Spotting	To have coloured spotting on a white body; spots to be clear, distinct and well-distributed all over the body including belly.	(30)
Feet Markings	To have solid colour covering the feet.	(10)
Colour	Colour to conform with ESCC, NACC or Argente Standards, as appropriate. Eye colour also to conform to these standards, except for the Black whose eyes may have a ruby tint.	10
Coat	To be soft & silky, clean and short, groomed free of guard hairs.	10
		100

incorrect, it describes the colour and health problems that they may have. This outcome can be completely avoided by adopting the practice of breeding a Dalmation to a non-Dalmation, usually a solid coloured guinea pig, to ensure that the babies can only inherit one Dalmation gene. Because the Dalmation gene is dominant, this mating will result in a theoretical ratio of 50% Dalmation and 50% non-Dalmation babies.

Dalmation

Roan

The Roan is a coloured guinea pig with white hairs mixed evenly throughout the body except on the head and feet which are solid coloured. This colour pattern is also seen in other animal species including horses and cattle.

They were first developed by crossing Roan Abyssinians to Self Blacks and then selective breeding was used to achieve the smooth coated variety. Like the Dalmation, they are now accepted in all recognised colours including Agouti and Argente.

The Roan gene works in a similar way to the Dalmation gene described above and is also dominant. The same practice of mating a Roan

DESIRED STANDARD		Points
Head, Eyes and Ears	Head to be short and broad, with a gently curving profile. Muzzle to be of good width and rounded at the nostrils. Eyes to be large, bright and bold and set with good width between. Ears to be large and drooping, and set with good width between.	15
Body Shape	To have short, cobby body with good width across shoulders and body. To be fit and of good substance, with plenty of firm flesh. To have good size appropriate to age.	10
Markings	To have a solid head and feet but white hairs to be evenly intermixed throughout the body.	60
Head Markings	To have solid colour with a clean demarcation line separating it from the body markings.	
Roaning	To have an even intermixing of white and coloured hairs all over the body, including the belly, to create a level appearance with no areas of shading.	
Feet Markings	To have solid colour covering the feet.	
Colour	Colour to conform to the recognised colours.	10
Coat	To be soft & silky, clean and short, groomed free of guard hairs.	5
		100

to a non-Roan is also advised to avoid the possibility of malformed babies.

Both the breeds described above are smooth coated exhibition varieties. The genes have also been bred into other types of guinea pig including longhaired and rough coated. Any guinea pig with a mixture of white and coloured markings on its body may be a Dalmation or Roan and thus the advice on breeding would apply similarly.

BELOW: *An inquisitive Roan.*

Roan

COLOURS

Roans may be exhibited in any of the colours that are standardised for Selfs (with the exception of white), Agoutis or Argentis.

BELOW: *Roan Strawberry*

ABOVE: *Roan Black*

Crested English / American / AOV

ABOVE: *Crested Himalayan*

The crested cavy can be any breed of smooth cavy with a crest on its forehead. The crest consists of a rosette radiating from a centre point between the eyes and ears. The crest should be deep and regular, with no areas of flatness, have a pin point centre and the lower edge should be well down to the nose. The American Crested has a crest of a contrasting colour.

ABOVE: *Crested American DE Golden*

Crested English / American / AOV

ENGLISH STANDARD

		Points
Head, Eyes and Ears	Head to be short and broad, with a gently curving profile. Muzzle to be of good width and rounded at the nostrils. Eyes to be large, bright and bold and set with good width between. Ears to be large and drooping, with lower rim parallel to the ground & set with good width between.	24
Crest	To radiate from a central point between the eyes and ears. To be a deep regular rosette with the lower edge well down to the nose. To have a pinpoint centre.	20
Body Shape	As self cavy.	20
Colour	As self cavy.	24
Coat	As self cavy.	12
		100

AMERICAN STANDARD

		Points
Head, Eyes and Ears		18
Crest	20 points here are for the crest having a complete circle of contrasting colour to the body colour.	40
Body Shape		15
Colour		18
Coat		9

AOV STANDARD

The standards for all the other AOV crested have 20 points for the crest and the rest of the points are allocated according to the standard of the breed which carries the crest.

ABOVE: *These English Crested cavies came first, second and third in show.*

ABOVE: *These American Crested cavies came first, second and third in their class.*

189

Solid Satin

The satin's most characteristic feature is the coat texture and particularly the sheen. Thus satin guinea pigs have a unique coat with a lustrous sheen. This is quite different from the normal glossy coat seen on a healthy smooth coated guinea pig and is caused by the shaft of each hair being hollow making them highly reflective. Satins are most commonly seen in smooth coated, solid coloured varieties.

They may be exhibited in any solid colour although these are not required to match exactly the English Self standard colours. The satin coat has an effect on colour, for example,

making a white coat appear ivory. They are popular in the paler colours as these show the 'satinisation' to its best advantage. The satin variation of marked or coated breeds may also be exhibited.

Although the Satin is a beautiful breed, it is important to be aware that some Satins can develop a degenerative bone disease called Osteodystrophy. Although a positive diagnosis can only be made by x-ray, the classic signs of weight loss and joint stiffness causing a bunny hopping gait may alert you to the fact that your pet needs veterinary attention.

ABOVE: *Satin DE Ivory*

Solid Satin

ABOVE: *Satin Ivory Sole*

ABOVE: *Satin Cream Gentil*

DESIRED STANDARD		Points
Head, Eyes and Ears	Roman nose with good width of muzzle, squared off at the end but rounded at the corners. Eyes to be large, bright and bold and set with good width between. Ears to be large and drooping, with lower rim parallel to the ground & set with good width between.	25
Body Shape	To have short, cobby body with deep, broad shoulders. Broad in body. To be fit and of good substance, with plenty of firm flesh. To have good size appropriate to age.	20
Satinisation	To show a distinct satin sheen that is pronounced and even on all body areas, able to 'catch' and reflect any light that is directed towards the coat.	30
Colour	To be of any solid colour, but to be even all over the body, although allowance must be made for the fact that shorter hair on the face and feet will reflect light differently and make colour appear darker than on the body. Undercolour to be carried well down to the skin. Pigmentation on ears, feet and nostrils to match body colour.	15
Coat	To be soft & silky, clean and short, groomed free of guard hairs.	10
		100

GUIDANCE NOTES

The Solid Satin is a solid-coloured cavy with a satinised coat, satinisation being due to hollow hair shafts in the coat. The satin sheen of the coat is of great importance. To assess the degree and quality of the sheen, judges should handle the cavy in such a way that the coat 'catches the light' to its fullest advantage. Satinisation imparts an extra intensity to any colour, so that exact compliance with shades in other varieties should not be expected.

Solid Satin

ABOVE: *Satin Golden Harris PE*

ABOVE: *Satin Buff Stroodle*

ABOVE: *Satin Golden DE*

Satin Non-Selfs

As well as the popular Solids Satins may be exhibited in any of the following Non-Self varieties:

Satin Agouti	Satin Bicolour
Satin Argente	Satin Tortoiseshell
Satin Dutch	Satin Brindle
Satin Himalayan	Satin Dalmation
Satin Tort & White	Satin Roan
Satin Tricolour	Satin Crested

GUIDANCE NOTES

In all cases, other than for Satin Cresteds, the Standard consists of 30 points for Satinisation, as for the Solid Satin, and 70% of the points for the corresponding Non-Self variety.

For Satin Cresteds the Standard consists of 30 points for Satinisation, as for the Solid Satin, 20 points for crest (formation) and 50% of the points for the corresponding Crested variety (including crest colour on American Cresteds).

Because satinisation affects coat quality in a fundamental way, due to the hollow hair shafts of the satin coat:
Satin versions of Standardised Coated varieties such as Abyssinian, Rex and all Longhairs will be recognised as and exhibited in Guide Standard classes only.

195

Emerging Breeds

The Rare Variety Cavy Club caters for all that is new in the Cavy World. That being the case it also deals with varieties of cavies that have not yet been fully recognised by the fancy and do not have a Full or Guide Standard. These breeds are in two categories:

1 Those which have been presented to the RVCC and granted support but not been given a Guide Standard yet.

2 Those which have not yet been presented to the RVCC or need extra work before they are granted support.

BELOW: *The Lunkyara has an extraordinary coat...*

Swiss
Sable
Lunkarya
Marten Sable
Chinchilla
Caramel

All of these breeds can be shown in special 'New Emerging Variety' classes at shows. Note, the above is not a full list of new breeds, by the very nature of the description, new breeds come along all the time.

... and a very pretty face!

Emerging Breeds

LEFT AND ABOVE: *These Lunkyara guinea pigs seem dwarfed by their own hair.*

Emerging Breeds

ABOVE: *Sable*

ABOVE: *Marten Sable*

ABOVE: *Caramel Self*

ABOVE: *Chinchilla*

Emerging Breeds

ABOVE: *Belted*
RIGHT: *Lakeland*
BELOW: *Harlequin Chocolate*

ABOVE: *Otter*
LEFT: *Magpie*
BELOW: *Ridge Back*

Index

A

Abbysinian 23, 100, 126
abscesses and cysts 82
ACS 62
Agouti 23, 103, 126, 136, 137
Agouti Chocolate 138
Agouti Cinnamon 138
Agouti Cream 137
Agouti Golden Dulcenayer 139
Agouti Golden Keisha 139
Agouti Lemon 140
Agouti Silver 140
Agouti Solid Gold 143
Agouti Solid Silver 142
Alpaca 24, 25, 121, 126
anus 67
apples 34, 53
Argente 126, 144, 145, 146
Argente Cream 145
Argente Golden 145
Argente Lilac 144

B

baby Satin boars 119
baby Shelties 118
baby vitamin drops 95
bananas 34
beetroot 32
Belted 202
Bicolour 126, 170, 171, 172, 173
birth 116, 117

bites 67
Black Fox 161
Black Himalayan 157
Black Self 135
bloat 82
boar 14, 16, 19, 20, 21
boar genitals 87
breed standards 98
breeds classification 126
breeder 19
Brindle 126, 178, 179
broccoli 32
Buff Self 133
Buff Self adult 101, 125
bumble foot 82

C

cabbage 32
cage 37, 38, 48
Cambridge Cavy Trust 70, 72
Caramel 197, 201
carrots 32, 35, 53
cats 42, 60, 70
cauliflower 32, 53
Cavia Porcellus 8
cavy/cavies 8, 12, 37, 42, 66, 98, 108, 109, 110
cavy pellets 33
celery 33
cereal mixes 31
cherries 34
chicory 32
Chinchilla 197, 201
chinchillas 12, 66

chinchilla grass pellets 75
chipmunks 66
Chocolate Dalmatian 7
Chocolate Himalayan 157
Chocolate Self 135
"chuttering" 14, 16
clover 34, 56
colds 82, 92
constipation 82
coprophagy 17
Coronet 24, 126
Cream Self 132
Crested 23, 126, 187
Crested American 187, 188, 189
Crested American Black 45
Crested American DE Golden 187
Crested English 187, 188, 189
Crested English Cream 59
Crested Himalayan 187
cucumber 32, 51
cultivated vegetables 32
curly kale 53
cystitis 84
cysts 84

D

Dalmation 23, 26, 126, 180, 181, 182, 183
dandelions 34, 53, 56, 84
diarrhea 84, 85

dogs 38, 40, 60, 70
Dutch 23, 126, 147, 148, 149, 150, 151
Dutch Black 147, 148
Dutch Chocolate 149, 151
Dutch Cream 151
Dutch Red 150

E

earache 73
ear drops 85
ears 67
emerging breeds 126, 196, 197, 198, 199, 200, 201, 202, 203, 204, 205
euthanasia 76
evaporated milk 121
eyes 65, 67

F

"The Fancy" 26
fatty eye 86, 87
feet 67
Fox 126, 162, 163
foxes 38, 40
free range 21
fruits 34
fungal mouth and throat infections 88

G

Gallagher, Julie 102
gerbils 66
Golden Agouti Solid 142

Golden Self DE 134
Golden Self PE 134
grapes 34
grass 34, 52, 56, 85
grazing ark 45
grease gland 12, 67, 70
grooming 69
Gs Belted 126
Gs Harlequin 126
Gs Magpie 126
Gs Ridgeback 126
Gs Standard Selfs 126
Gs Teddy 126
Gurney, Peter 26, 70

H
hair 12, 65, 67
"hairy" Alpaca 26
hamsters 66
hand rearing 121
Harlequin Chocolate 202
hay 31, 45, 46
hay seed 86
heatstroke 89
herbivore 30, 58
Himalayan 24, 156, 157,
   158, 159, 160, 161
Himalayan Black 160
Himalayan Chocolate
   160
hutch 37, 44

I
impacted rectum 88
Incas 8, 10
Indoor Free Rangers 45

JKL
Lakeland 202
lettuce 33
lice 77
Lilac Fox 161
litter tray 46
log 44
Longhaired Merino 102
loose droppings 67
lumps 67
Lunkyara 196, 197, 199

M
mange 77
Magpie 204
Marten Sable 29, 197,
   200
mating 114
maze 45
melon 34
Merino 24, 126
mice 66
mites 79
motions 121
mouth 69
mouth scabs 88
mycosis 78

N
nail clipping 68
National Cavy Club 26
Non-Selfs 23
nose 69

O
Oldies 76

oranges 34
Otter 204

P
paracetamol 73
paralyzed back legs 91
parasites 69
parsley 34, 56, 84
parsnips 32
peapods 32
pearl barley water 84
pears 34, 53
penis 69
peppers, red and green
   33
Peru 10
Peruvians 5, 24, 46, 51,
   104, 126
pet shop 18
Piggy Potions 72, 84
plantain 34
pneumonia 45
poisonous plants (wild
   and garden) 35
post natal sores 92
potato peelings 33
pregnancy 115

R
rabbit hutch 48
rabbits 62, 65, 66
Rare Variety Cavy Club
   196
rats 38, 66
rehydration salts 85
Rex 23, 100, 126

Ridge Back 204
Roan 23, 26, 126, 184,
   185, 186
Roan Black 186
Roan Strawberry 186
rodents 8
runner beans 32
running lice 77

S
Sable 197, 200
Saffron Self 133
salad vegetables 32
sarcoptic mange 77
Satin 23
Satin Buff Stroodle 194
Satin Cream Gentil 192
Satin DE Ivory 191
Satin Golden DE 195
Satin Golden Harris PE
   194
Satin Ivory Sole 192
Satin Non-Self 126, 195
Scottish National Cavy
   Club 26
scurvy 92, 94
Self Cavy 128, 129, 130,
   131, 132, 133
Selfs 20, 22, 100
shampooing 70, 81
Sheltie 24, 83, 126
Shepherd's Purse 34, 85
Showing 98
skin 69
skin problems 77
snuffles 95

Solid Agouti 126, 141, 142, 143
Solid Satin 126, 190, 191, 193, 194
Southern Cavy Club 26
sow 14, 19, 21, 122
sow genitals 87
Sow thistle 34
spinach 32
spring greens 53
sprout tops and stalks 32
squirrels 12
Stanley-Spatcher, Vedra 72
static lice 77
stoats 38
strawberry leaves 34
stress 61
stud 21

swaddling 72
swede 32
sweetcorn 32
Swiss 59, 197
syringe feeding 75, 121

T

Tan 126, 164, 165, 166, 167, 168, 169
Tan Beige 164
Tan Black 165
Tan Chocolate 167
Tan Lilac 165
Tan Slate 168
Tan Slate Nat Fox 168
teeth 69
temperature 57
Texel 24, 25, 104, 126
tomatoes 33

tonic 73
tooth problems 95
Tortoise and White 152, 153, 154, 155
Tortoiseshell 23, 126, 176, 177
Tortoiseshell-and-white 23, 126
Tricolour 126, 174, 175
tummy ache 73
tunnels 45, 49
turnips 32

U

urine 121

V

vegetable matter 30
vet 70

Vick 92
Vitamin C 30, 31, 53, 63, 84, i94

W

"war dance" 14, 15
water 32, 44
weasels 38
weight 69
"wheeping" 13, 14, 51, 52
White Self PE 132
wild plants 34
wood shavings 44
wounds 97
wrapping 112, 113